LEITHS

HOW TO COOK
CAKES

JENNY STRINGER   CLAIRE MACDONALD
CAMILLA SCHNEIDEMAN

Photography by Peter Cassidy

Quadrille
PUBLISHING

CONTENTS

NOTES

✻ All spoon measures are level unless otherwise stated:
1 tsp = 5ml spoon; 1 tbsp = 15ml spoon.

✻ Use medium eggs unless otherwise suggested. Anyone
who is pregnant or in a vulnerable health group should avoid
recipes that use raw egg whites or lightly cooked eggs.

✻ Use fresh herbs unless otherwise suggested.

✻ If using the zest of citrus fruit, buy unwaxed fruit.

✻ Timings are guidelines for conventional ovens. If you
are using a fan-assisted oven, set your oven temperature
approximately 15°C (1 Gas mark) lower. Use an oven
thermometer to check the temperature.

INTRODUCTION

Baking cakes can be so rewarding. Not only are the results fairly swift and sweet, they are perfect for sharing and consequently gathering appreciation and praise. All cooks, from beginner to expert, can follow instructions and achieve a delicious result.

Baking does involve paying close attention to detail and more careful weighing than most other areas of cooking, however this does not spell the end to creativity or mean only those who slavishly follow instruction will succeed. Rather find the recipes that suit your cooking style, and flavours you love, and use these as a basis to experiment.

There are always variables in cooking, and the unpredictable nature of the domestic oven does present a challenge when giving accurate cooking times. Most manufacturers say the actual temperature of the oven may vary up to 20°C from the temperature you have chosen on the dial, and some we have used vary even more. We have also found oven thermometers available for domestic use to be pretty erratic.

However, we cannot all use the technology available in professional patisseries. The important thing is to learn what to look for, so how to tell the cake is ready without simply relying on a kitchen timer.

In this book we aim to give you the confidence to make the decision to remove the cake or cookie at the perfect moment. And of course, how to mix, whisk, beat and stir most effectively so that you can master all the skills in the baker's repertoire and produce light cakes of pure perfection.

GETTING STARTED

THE OVEN
Turn on the oven in good time so that it will have reached the required temperature before you are ready to put the cake in. If the oven temperature is too low, and still heating up, this will have an effect on the rise of the cake.

The correct temperature is calculated to set the mixture without melted fat running out, loss of air bubbles, or sugar burning, depending on the recipe in question.

We use gas ovens at Leiths School of Food and Wine, but our recipes have also been tested in a variety of domestic ovens. When baking in electric fan ovens, you should reduce the temperature by 10–20°C, or cakes tend to emerge a little dry. It is also possible to reduce the temperature for the last quarter of the cooking time, again by 10–20°C to prevent over-browning. However, cakes do need a blast of heat at the beginning of the process to make them rise and set. If it is possible to turn the fan off in your oven then do so, as this will prevent the cake from drying out.

It is generally a good idea to allow a cake to have at least half of its cooking time before disturbing it by opening the oven door. In all honesty a little peep probably won't hurt, but fully opening the door may do so. Allowing a gust of cooler air in can cause a cake to sink and the oven to lose heat, resulting in a dense cake.

Unless a recipe states otherwise, move the oven shelf to the middle of the oven when you start to heat the oven. Even in fan ovens, the middle is a good place to bake a cake as it is most likely to have an even surrounding heat. Moving the shelf in advance means you can be far swifter when putting the cake into the oven and less likely to cause the oven temperature to drop as it goes in.

The more things you cook in the oven at one time, the longer the cooking time, so if you are baking several trays of cookies, you may need to adjust the cooking times to accommodate this, and to swap their position in the oven halfway through cooking to ensure even cooking.

Ingredients

You will find your baking becomes more proficient when you understand what role each ingredient plays in the process.

TEMPERATURE OF INGREDIENTS

It is best to use ingredients at room temperature for baking. Fat traps air bubbles if it is pliable but not melted and greasy, and so the eggs should be room temperature too or they will cool the butter down and stop it trapping air as effectively. Cold eggs can also cause the butter to curdle the mixture. Also, incorporating air bubbles into eggs is more effective when they are at room temperature.

FAT

The fat in cakes is important for flavour and also for the cake's keeping properties. Butter gives the best flavour. You can use either unsalted or standard (salted) butter, though many people prefer the flavour of unsalted in cakes. In some recipes unsalted butter is specified to control the salt element of the recipe. Soft baking margarine can help make a very speedy cake with an excellent texture, but do check the packet, as some brands are unsuitable. Both butter and margarine trap air bubbles when they are creamed with sugar, one of the ways in which creamed cakes rise. Oils are sometimes used in cakes, but as they don't trap any air, the cakes have a dense, almost fudgy texture.

FLOUR

Plain flour is the most commonly used flour in cake making, sometimes with measured raising agents added to it. Self-raising flour already has a standard amount of raising agent added and is often used in creamed cakes. Both plain and self-raising flours are lower in gluten than strong bread flour, which helps to keep the crumb tender. If a recipe calls for self-raising flour when you only have plain, you can make your own by adding 2 level tsp baking powder to 225g plain flour. Brown flour can be used, but as it doesn't trap air bubbles as well as the finer white, the cakes tend to be heavier. Using one quarter brown and three quarters white flour can be a workable compromise between lightness and fibre.

RAISING AGENTS

Air is added to a cake mixture by beating, whisking and sifting. However, the most dramatic leavening effect is produced by adding raising agents. This is where the culinary chemistry occurs. An acid and alkali react to produce air bubbles, which are then trapped in the mixture that happens to be the perfect consistency to contain them. The cake sets in the heat of the oven before the bubbles are able to rise up and escape, so the result is a network of bubbles in the cooked sponge.

It is important to sift the raising agents into the other dry ingredients to ensure they are evenly distributed for an even rise. They also have rather a soapy flavour, so you want to avoid lumps. Most raising agents start working as soon as they come into contact with liquid so, without panicking, do make sure you have prepared the oven and all the remaining ingredients so that the mixture can go into the oven as soon as possible after the raising agents are activated.

The most common added raising agent is baking powder, which is a mixture of the alkaline bicarbonate of soda and an acid. Bicarbonate of soda can be used alone, as it will release gas when mixed with water, but works faster when the mixture is made acidic, for example with lemon juice.

EGGS

Medium eggs, weighing approximately 55g in the shell, are used in this book. If using large eggs, leave out a couple of teaspoons of the beaten egg. If you need to bring refrigerated eggs to room temperature quickly, put the whole eggs in a bowl of warm (not hot) water for a few minutes before use.

SUGAR

As well as sweetening the mixture, sugar helps to stop gluten in the flour toughening the cake. Creamed and whisked cakes need a fine-grained sugar such as caster or golden caster. Golden caster sugar can be used in place of standard caster sugar in any recipe. It will add a subtle caramel colour and flavour to your cakes.

Darker, more highly flavoured sugars and syrups like muscovado and treacle are used to provide deep flavour that can mask the taste of raising agents in melted cakes such as gingerbread. Molasses is used in this way and, as an alkali, also reacts with the acidity of the raising agent to create air bubbles. If you have no caster sugar, coarser grained sugars such as granulated or demerara can be ground to a finer grain in a blender.

LIQUID

Many cakes, particularly creamed cakes, may require a little added liquid to bring them to the perfect consistency. Water can be used to loosen all cake mixtures and milk is suitable for creamed cakes. Whisked cakes sometimes require a little liquid to be added to the eggs and sugar to help the sugar melt and the mixture to trap the necessary amount of air.

SEPARATING EGGS

1 To separate an egg, crack the egg on the edge of a table or use a cutlery knife. Avoid too much pressure or you will break the egg in half. You only want to crack the shell. Carefully ease apart the shell halves over a medium to large bowl. Some white will fall into the bowl; it is important that none of the yolk does.

2 Carefully pass the yolk between the half shells, encouraging the white to fall into the bowl. Once all or most of the white is in the bowl, all that may be left on the yolk is the 'chalaza', or thread. Carefully prise this away from the yolk, with the edge of a shell so it falls into the bowl. Put the yolk into a small bowl.

WHISKING EGG WHITES

Egg whites should be whisked just as they are needed. If whisked in advance, the air bubbles will burst and the whites will lose volume. To achieve more stable whisked whites, start whisking slowly to create small bubbles of air, then gradually increase the speed of whisking. As more air is incorporated, the consistency of the egg whites will change. Egg whites are used at different stages of whisking for different purposes, so it helps to be able to recognise the consistency at different stages.

Egg whites should be whisked in scrupulously clean bowls, free from any fat, which can impede whisking. A copper bowl is ideal. Otherwise, choose stainless steel or glass, but avoid plastic bowls which tend to trap grease.

Generally, unless otherwise specified, egg whites should be whisked to the same consistency as the mixture to which they are being added. Like consistencies will combine more easily and efficiently with minimal loss of volume.

Using a large, fine balloon whisk, start to whisk the egg whites. As air is incorporated they will become slightly foamy, opaque and very thin. They will increase in volume as you continue to whisk, becoming white and foamy. If you lift the whisk vertically up and turn it upside down, the whites will fall from the whisk.

SOFT PEAK Continue whisking and the whites will become paler and stiffer. Test them again by lifting the balloon whisk vertically, then turning the whisk upside down. If the whites cling to the whisk and start to create a 'peak', but the peak falls over on itself, the egg whites are at the soft peak stage.

MEDIUM PEAK Whisk for a little longer then test again by lifting the whisk; the whites will cling to the whisk and, as it is pulled up vertically and turned upside down, they will start to fall over onto themselves, then stop halfway. This is the medium peak stage, used for soufflés and mousses.

STIFF PEAK Continue to whisk again; the whites will become very stiff and when tested the peak will hold its vertical position and not fall over on itself. This is known as the stiff peak stage. At this stage there is still some elasticity in the whites.

PREPARING CAKE TINS

Cake tins need to be lightly oiled or lined with a non-stick paper to stop the cake sticking to the tin and to give the outside of the cake a delicious thin crust.

A flavourless cooking oil such as sunflower can be used, or butter, and even lard, but a very fine layer is essential or the outside of the cake will seem to be 'fried' and greasy round the edges. Wiping a butter paper around the inside of a tin or over the lining paper is effective, or you could apply melted butter thinly with a pastry brush to ensure a fine layer.

Greaseproof paper or baking parchment are specified for lining tins in the recipes that follow, and they can be used interchangeably. Baking parchment has superior non-stick qualities, but it is sometimes easier to line a cake tin with greaseproof paper, as it is a little absorbent and so sticks

better to the tin. Be aware that greaseproof paper, if not oiled, can stick to the cake and prove tricky to peel off.

Tins for different types of cakes are traditionally prepared in differing ways, as some cakes need more protection from the oven heat, are more prone to sticking, or require a sweeter crust than others.

It is important to use the tin size specified in the recipe, as it does make a difference how deep the mixture is when it is baked. However, if you do not have a tin of the right size, try to use a tin where the mixture comes at least half to two thirds of the way up the sides.

TO BASE-LINE A ROUND TIN
For 2 tins, fold a piece of greaseproof paper in half and place a tin on top. Use a pencil to trace around the outside of the tin, then cut inside the line of the circle and trim to size if necessary.

Brush the paper with melted butter. Lightly brush the tins with melted butter and lay a disc of greaseproof paper in the bottom of each tin. The disc should be cut to size; if it comes up the side of the tin it will prevent the cake having a clean, neat edge.

FOR A WHISKED SPONGE
Grease the tin and place a disc of greaseproof paper on the base, then grease it again. Dust with caster sugar, shaking it around the tin to coat it evenly, tap out the excess, then dust it with flour and tap out the excess.

TO LINE A LOAF TIN
Grease the tin, then line the base and short sides with a long strip of greaseproof paper that extends up over the sides. This makes it easier to remove the cake from the tin, by lifting the greaseproof paper ends.

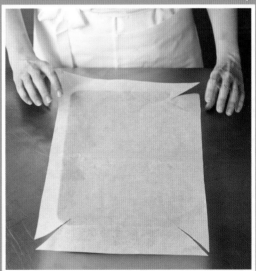

TO LINE A SHALLOW RECTANGULAR OR SQUARE TIN
To fully line a tin (for brownies, etc.), take a piece of baking parchment about 5cm bigger on all sides than the tin. Cut diagonally through the corners, about 5cm deep and lay the parchment in the roasting tin, pushing it into the corners. The cuts made through the corners will allow the paper to overlap neatly and line the tin.

TO LINE A DEEP ROUND TIN

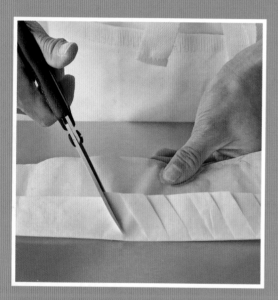

1 Cut 2 discs of greaseproof paper to fit the bottom of the tin. For the sides, fold a sheet of greaseproof paper in half lengthways, long enough to fit snugly inside the tin all the way round the inside. On the folded edge, fold up about 3cm again. Then, using scissors, make diagonal cuts across the 3cm depth of the folded border all the way along the paper.

2 Lightly grease the inside of the tin, lay a disc of greaseproof paper on the base, then fit the long sheet around the inside of the tin, with the border folded in, towards the middle of the tin. The cuts will overlap to allow you to line the sides of the tin neatly. Make sure the paper fits well into the bottom edge of the tin and trim the top if it protrudes too much over the rim. Place the second greaseproof paper disc on top. Lightly grease the paper base and sides.

A note on lining a tin for a rich fruit cake...

✳ As fruit cakes are dense and take a long time to cook, it is a good idea to wrap 2 or 3 layers of newspaper around the outside of the cake tin and tie them securely with kitchen string. This will help prevent the outside of the cake from overcooking during the lengthy cooking time.

1

CREAMED CAKES

The classic creamed cake is a Victoria sandwich. All manner of flavours and ingredients can be added to this basic mixture to create an endless variety of cakes. Once mastered, the classic sponge leads to more advanced recipes, and the opportunity for creativity.

To make the perfect creamed cake, make sure that the ingredients are at room temperature, the tin is prepared and the oven is heating before you begin to make the mixture. There are three main areas to concentrate on: creaming the butter and sugar until really pale, light and fluffy, beating well between each egg addition, and folding in the flour as carefully and gently as possible, to avoid losing the precious air that has been incorporated.

The cake rises because of the raising agent in the self-raising flour, the air incorporated during the creaming of the butter and sugar, from sifting the flour and beating in the eggs, and also because of the steam created in the oven heat from water in the eggs.

VICTORIA SANDWICH

MAKES a 20cm round cake

Oil, to grease
225g butter, softened
225g caster sugar,
    plus extra to dust

4 eggs, at room temperature
225g self-raising flour
1–2 tbsp water or milk
5–7 tbsp raspberry jam

The traditional Victoria sandwich uses equal weights of butter, sugar, eggs and flour. It is a classic teatime favourite. You will need two 20cm sandwich tins.

1 Heat the oven to 180°C/gas mark 4. Lightly brush the 2 sandwich tins with a little oil and line the base of each with a disc of greaseproof paper.

2 Using a wooden spoon or hand-held electric whisk, cream the butter and sugar together in a medium bowl until pale, light and fluffy. The paler the mixture becomes, the more air has been incorporated, which helps to create a lighter cake.

3 Break the eggs into a small bowl and beat lightly with a fork until broken up. Gradually add the egg to the creamed butter and sugar, in several additions and beating well after each. Adding eggs that are too cold, or adding them too quickly, can cause the mixture to curdle. If this happens, add 1 tbsp of the flour to help to stabilise the mixture.

4 Once all the egg has been added, sift the flour over the surface of the mixture and fold it in, using a large metal spoon.

5 Check that the mixture is at the correct dropping consistency (see right). If a little too thick, fold in 1–2 tbsp water or milk.

6 Divide the mixture between the prepared tins and smooth the tops using a spatula. Bake in the middle of the oven for about 20–30 minutes, or until well risen and golden. The cakes should feel spongy to the fingertips and not leave an indentation when pressed gently.

7 Allow to cool for a few minutes in the tins, then turn the cakes out onto a wire rack and allow to cool completely before peeling off the lining paper.

8 While the cakes are cooling, put the jam into a small saucepan over a low heat and gently warm through, to make it more spreadable. Sandwich the cooled cakes, bases together, with the jam and dust the top of the cake with caster sugar.

Variations

✳ **Coffee walnut cake** Dissolve 4 tsp good quality instant coffee granules in 1 tbsp warm water and stir into the mixture before you add the flour. Stir in 75g coarsely chopped walnuts after the flour. You may not need water or milk to achieve a dropping consistency. Omit the raspberry jam. Use coffee butter icing (see page 152) to sandwich and ice the top of the cake.

✳ **West Country sponge** Use golden caster sugar and add 1 tsp vanilla extract to the beaten eggs before beating into the mixture. Omit the jam. Stir 2 tsp icing sugar into 200g clotted cream and spread over the bottom cake layer. Slice 200–300g washed, hulled strawberries and arrange over the cream. Sandwich with the top cake layer and dust with icing sugar before serving.

A note on dropping consistency...

✳ A mixture at the correct dropping consistency contains just the right amount of liquid to produce a moist cake, and also to create the necessary steam to help the mixture rise. Too wet a mixture will prevent the cake rising well, as it won't trap the air bubbles effectively. To check the mixture is the correct dropping consistency, lift a spoonful up out of the bowl, turn the spoon and tap the handle on the side of the bowl. The mixture should drop reluctantly from the spoon – neither pouring off nor continuing to stick to the spoon.

STEP 2 Creaming the softened butter and sugar together, using a hand-held electric whisk, until pale, light and fluffy.

STEP 3 Gradually whisking the beaten egg into the creamed mixture, in several additions.

STEP 4 Carefully folding the flour into the mixture, using a large metal spoon.

STEP 5 Checking that the mixture is at the correct dropping consistency; i.e. it will drop reluctantly from the spoon.

(Continued overleaf)

Testing to see if the cake is cooked...

✳ A cooked creamed cake will be shrinking slightly away from the sides of the tin. Press lightly with a fingertip to make sure there is a spongy set all over the surface and your finger does not leave an indentation.

You can also test it by inserting a skewer into the centre of the cake; it should come out clean or with just a few moist crumbs clinging to it, but certainly no uncooked mixture.

Most cakes will take on a light golden brown colour when they are cooked, and the smell of a cooked cake is unmistakable.

Removing the cake from the tin...

✳ Allow the cake to stand in the tin for a minute or two before removing from the tin, unless the recipe states otherwise, or there is a risk of the cake collapsing a little. For creamed cakes, run a cutlery knife around the edge of the tin before trying to remove it. Make sure the flat of the knife is pressed against the tin as you do so and doesn't cut into the cake itself.

Cutting a cake into layers...

✳ It can be tricky to achieve straight layers of an even thickness when cutting a cake horizontally. It helps to use a long serrated knife, such as a bread knife. Place the cake on a board and score around the edge with the knife, then cut from one edge only as far as the middle. Give the cake a quarter turn, then cut from the edge to the middle again, and repeat.

Note that creamed cakes are usually cooked in sandwich tins, then layered with a filling, though they can be cooked in one tin, then split into layers. Whisked cakes are generally cooked in one tin and cut into layers.

Rescuing a curdled mixture...

✳ A creamed cake mixture curdles when the ingredients cease to be emulsified. This happens when the fat becomes too cold and so sets as small lumps rather than remaining blended with the other ingredients, or the liquid (in this case, the egg) is added too fast to emulsify with the fat. A cake made with a curdled mixture will have a slightly heavier texture. Beating in a tablespoonful of the measured flour will make the mixture smooth again, but this will make the texture not quite as light. However, if the cake is well made and baked it is unlikely that anyone will notice!

STRAWBERRY CAKE
WITH CREAM CHEESE ICING

SERVES 12–15

Oil, to grease
4 large eggs, at room
  temperature
180g unsalted butter,
  softened
350g caster sugar
1 tsp vanilla extract
2–4 tbsp milk
285g plain flour
4 tsp baking powder
Pinch of salt

FOR THE PURÉE
450g ripe strawberries
3 tsp caster sugar

FOR THE ICING
200g butter, softened
225g cream cheese
250g icing sugar
2 tsp lemon juice

TO ASSEMBLE
400g ripe strawberries

This is a lovely cake to make in the summer when home-grown strawberries are plentiful, ripe and sweet – perfect to feed a crowd. Serve it with a bowl of fresh berries on the side. If possible, macerate the strawberries for the fresh purée a day ahead to allow time for them to release their juices. You will need two 24cm round cake tins.

1 For the purée, roughly chop the strawberries, add to a bowl with the sugar, toss to coat and cover with cling film. Chill in the fridge for at least 2 hours, or ideally overnight, until the strawberries release most of their juices.

2 Blend the soaked strawberries with their juice in a food processor, in short pulses until they become a smooth purée; set aside. This purée will be used for both the cake and the icing.

3 For the icing, put the butter in a bowl and, using an electric whisk, mix until light, pale and fluffy, then add the cream cheese and mix until well combined. Sift in the icing sugar, a little at a time, on the slowest speed. Once incorporated, stir in the lemon juice and 60–90ml strawberry purée (enough to give a good flavour but ensuring the icing will be firm enough once chilled to be spreadable). Firm up in the fridge for about 1 hour.

4 Heat the oven to 180°C/gas mark 4. Oil the 2 cake tins and line the base of each with a disc of greaseproof paper, then lightly oil the paper again (see page 10).

5 For the cake, separate the eggs (see page 8). Using an electric whisk, cream together the butter and sugar in a large bowl until light and fluffy. Add the egg yolks, vanilla, 2 tbsp milk and the remaining strawberry purée (about 180ml). Combine well.

6 Sift the dry ingredients over the surface of the creamed mixture and fold in, using a large metal spoon or a spatula, until fully combined. Add up to 2 more tbsp of the milk, if needed, to give a dropping consistency (see page 16).

7 In a large, clean bowl, whisk the egg whites to stiff peaks (see page 9), using an electric whisk. Gently fold them into the cake mixture until combined, being careful not to over-mix.

8 Divide the cake mixture evenly between the 2 tins and bake in the middle of the oven for 35–45 minutes until a skewer inserted into the centre comes out clean, or with just a few moist crumbs clinging to it. Leave to cool in the tins for about 10 minutes, then turn out onto a wire rack, remove the lining paper and leave to cool completely.

9 Slice the strawberries carefully and set aside enough of the most perfect slices to cover the top of the cake in a single layer.

10 To assemble the cake, spread a quarter of the icing over the bottom cooled cake and top with a layer of strawberry slices, then sandwich the 2 cakes together. Spread the remaining icing evenly over the top and sides of the cake and decorate the top of the cake with the reserved strawberry slices.

ALMOND, HONEY AND YOGURT CAKE

SERVES 8–10

Oil, to grease
170g unsalted butter, softened
170g caster sugar
2 eggs, plus 1 extra yolk, at room temperature
100g fine semolina
100g plain flour
50g ground almonds
1 tsp baking powder
¼ tsp salt
½ tsp vanilla extract
3 tbsp honey
170g Greek yoghurt

FOR THE SYRUP
1 lemon
120g caster sugar
100ml water
1 tbsp honey

This cake can be made up to 3 days in advance and stored, well wrapped, in an airtight container. Try adding chopped dried apricots or other nuts to the mixture, such as pistachios or toasted hazelnuts, or add rosewater or orange flower water to the syrup for a Middle Eastern flavour. The cake is particularly delicious served warm with Greek yoghurt. You will need a 20cm round cake tin.

1 Heat the oven to 180°C/gas mark 4. Oil the cake tin, line the base with a disc of greaseproof paper, then lightly brush with a little more oil, including the sides (see page 10).

2 Put the butter and sugar in a medium bowl and cream together until light and fluffy, using an electric whisk or wooden spoon.

3 Break the eggs and extra yolk into a small bowl and beat lightly, using a fork, until broken up. Gradually beat the eggs into the creamed mixture, making sure each addition of egg is incorporated before adding the next.

4 Sift the semolina, flour, ground almonds, baking powder and salt over the surface and fold into the creamed mixture, using a large metal spoon or spatula. Fold in the vanilla, honey and yoghurt. The batter should be quite thick.

5 Pour the mixture into the prepared tin and bake in the middle of the oven for 45–55 minutes, or until rich golden brown, and a skewer inserted into the centre comes out clean, or with only a few moist crumbs clinging to it.

6 Meanwhile, to prepare the syrup, finely grate the lemon zest. Bring the sugar, water, honey and lemon zest to a simmer in a small saucepan. Reduce by half, to create a viscous syrup.

7 Once the cake is cooked, remove it from the oven and, while still warm, prick the sponge a few times, right through to the base, using a skewer. Pour over two thirds of the syrup and leave to cool in the tin for 20 minutes.

8 Transfer the cake to a serving plate and pour the remaining syrup over the top just before serving.

LUSCIOUS CHOCOLATE CAKE

SERVES 10–12

Oil, to grease
225g butter, softened
110g caster sugar
110g soft light brown sugar
4 eggs, at room temperature
170g self-raising flour
55g good quality dark
 cocoa powder
½ tsp baking powder
1–2 tbsp water or milk

FOR THE CHOCOLATE GANACHE
350g good quality dark
 chocolate, minimum
 60% cocoa solids
250ml double cream

Here, the addition of brown sugar and cocoa powder to a plain Victoria sandwich mixture transforms it into a scrumptious chocolate cake. There are lots of different cocoa powders available and you will really taste the difference in this cake if you use a good quality one. You will need two 20cm sandwich tins.

1 Heat the oven to 180°C/gas mark 4. Oil the 2 sandwich tins and line the base of each with a disc of greaseproof paper. Lightly brush with a little more oil, including the sides of the tin (see page 10).

2 Cream the butter and both sugars together in a medium bowl until paler, light and fluffy.

3 Break the eggs into a small bowl and beat lightly, using a fork, until broken up. Gradually add the egg in several additions, beating well after each addition.

4 Sift over the flour, cocoa powder and baking powder, and fold in carefully. Add enough of the water or milk to give a dropping consistency (see page 16).

5 Divide the mixture between the prepared tins and smooth the tops with a spatula. Bake in the middle of the oven for 20–30 minutes, or until the cakes are well risen, feel spongy to the fingertips and do not leave an indentation when pressed gently.

6 Remove from the oven and leave to cool for a few minutes in the tins before turning out onto a wire rack. Leave to cool completely before peeling off the greaseproof paper.

7 Meanwhile, to make the ganache, chop the chocolate into small, 1cm pieces, and place in a heatproof bowl. Bring the cream to a simmer in a small saucepan over a medium heat, then pour it over the chocolate and stir gently until the chocolate has melted and the ingredients are well combined.

8 Allow the ganache to cool until it begins to thicken a little around the edges, then beat with electric beaters on a slow speed for 1–2 minutes until thickened a little, but still creamy. Do not aerate the mixture too much.

9 When the cakes have cooled completely, sandwich them together with a quarter of the ganache and spread the remainder over the top and sides of the cake, smoothing it out with a palette knife. Cut into slices to serve.

CHOCOLATE CARAMEL ESPRESSO CAKE

SERVES 10–12

Oil, to grease
85g good quality dark
   chocolate, minimum
   60% cocoa solids
1 tsp vanilla extract
340g soft light brown sugar
290ml milk
110g butter, softened
2 eggs, at room temperature
75ml espresso coffee
225g plain flour
1 tsp bicarbonate of soda

FOR THE FILLING
397g tin of caramel
   (dulce de leche)

FOR THE ICING
65g good quality dark
   chocolate, minimum
   60% cocoa solids
100g unsalted butter,
   softened
200g icing sugar
20g good quality dark
   cocoa powder
Few drops of vanilla extract
25ml strong espresso coffee

You will need two 20cm sandwich tins.

1 Heat the oven to 190°C/gas mark 5. Lightly brush the base of the 2 sandwich tins with oil and line the base of each with a disc of greaseproof paper. Lightly brush with a little more oil, including the sides (see page 10).

2 Break the chocolate into small pieces and put in a heavy-based saucepan with the vanilla, half the sugar and half the milk. Melt over a low heat, stirring until smooth. Remove from the heat and set aside to cool.

3 Put the butter and remaining sugar in a large bowl and, using an electric whisk, beat until light and fluffy. Break the eggs into a small bowl and, using a fork, beat lightly to break them up. Add the eggs to the creamed mixture in several additions, beating well between each addition, then stir in the chocolate mixture and the espresso.

4 Sift the flour and bicarbonate of soda over the surface and fold in carefully and thoroughly. Stir in the remaining milk; the mixture should be the consistency of a thick batter.

5 Divide the mixture between the 2 tins and bake in the middle of the oven for 35–40 minutes. When cooked, the cakes should feel spongy to the touch and should be evenly set.

6 Remove from the oven and leave to cool in the tins for a few minutes before turning out onto a wire rack. Peel off the greaseproof paper and leave to cool completely.

7 Meanwhile, to make the icing, break the chocolate into small pieces and put into a heatproof bowl. Set the bowl over a saucepan of just-boiled water, ensuring the bowl is not touching the water, and leave to melt, giving it an occasional stir to encourage it. When the chocolate has completely melted, remove the bowl from the pan and set aside to cool.

8 Whisk the butter in a medium bowl, using an electric whisk, until light and fluffy. Sift the icing sugar and cocoa powder into a separate bowl, then gradually add to the butter, with the electric whisk still running. Stir in the melted chocolate and the vanilla, then beat in the espresso until smooth.

9 To assemble, cut each cooled cake into 2 layers (see page 19). Set aside the best layer for the top, then spread the others with the caramel. Stack up the cakes to make a 4-layered cake.

10 Spread the icing over the top and around the sides of the cake, using a palette knife and swirl the top decoratively with the knife. Chill briefly to set the icing if necessary, before cutting into slices to serve.

CINNAMON AND SOURED CREAM CAKE WITH PINE NUTS

SERVES 8–10

Oil or melted butter, to grease
285g plain flour, plus extra
  to dust
140g unsalted butter,
  softened
225g caster sugar
3 eggs, at room temperature
1 tsp vanilla extract
300ml soured cream

2 tsp ground cinnamon
1½ tsp baking powder
1 tsp bicarbonate soda
Pinch of salt

FOR THE NUT MIXTURE
85g pine nuts
40g soft light brown sugar
1 tsp ground cinnamon

This cake is equally delicious made with flaked almonds in place of the pine nuts, and is perfect to enjoy with coffee. You will need a 23cm round loose-based cake tin.

1 Heat the oven to 180°C/gas mark 4. Lightly grease the cake tin, line the base with a disc of greaseproof paper, grease again and dust with flour (see pages 10–11).

2 To make the nut mixture, mix together the pine nuts, soft light brown sugar and cinnamon in a medium bowl, and set aside.

3 In a large bowl, cream together the butter and caster sugar, using an electric whisk or wooden spoon, until light and fluffy. Break the eggs into a small bowl and, using a fork, beat lightly to break them up, then gradually add to the creamed mixture, beating well between each addition. Beat in the vanilla and soured cream.

4 Sift over the flour, cinnamon, baking powder, bicarbonate of soda and salt and, using a large metal spoon or a spatula, fold in until fully incorporated. The mixture will be quite thick.

5 Spoon half the mixture into the prepared tin, then sprinkle over half the nut mixture. Cover with the remaining cake mixture and sprinkle over the remaining nut mixture.

6 Bake in the middle of the oven for 50 minutes, or until a skewer inserted into the centre comes out clean. Check after 30 minutes that the nuts on the top are not browning too much; if they are, place a piece of foil or damp greaseproof paper over the top of the tin.

7 When cooked, remove from the oven and leave to cool for a few minutes in the tin, before removing the cake from the tin. Peel off the lining paper and leave to cool on a wire rack.

GINGER AND CARDAMOM BUTTERMILK CAKE

Oil, to grease
30g preserved stem ginger in syrup
1 tbsp stem ginger syrup (from the jar)
100ml buttermilk
100ml milk
1 orange
110g butter, softened

250g golden caster or soft light brown sugar
3 eggs
220g plain flour
2 tsp baking powder
2 tsp ground cardamom
1½ tsp ground mixed spice
1 tsp ground ginger
30g ground pistachio nuts

Ground pistachios are not easily obtainable, but you can grind your own using a spice grinder or the small bowl of a food processor. It is easier to grind a large quantity, enough to cover the blades, and any leftover can be stored in an airtight container. Alternatively, you could use ground almonds. You will need a 24cm round springform cake tin.

1 Heat the oven to 180°C/gas mark 4. Oil the springform cake tin and line the base and sides with baking parchment (see page 12).

2 Finely chop the stem ginger and place in a small bowl with the syrup, buttermilk and milk. Finely grate the orange zest and squeeze the juice, then stir both into the buttermilk mixture and set aside.

3 Using an electric whisk or wooden spoon, cream the butter and sugar together in a medium bowl until pale and fluffy.

4 Break the eggs into a small bowl and, using a fork, beat lightly to break them up. Add the eggs to the creamed mixture in several additions, beating well between each addition. Stir in the orange and buttermilk mixture.

5 Sift the flour, baking powder and spices into another bowl. Stir in the ground pistachios and, using a large metal spoon or a spatula, fold the dry ingredients into the creamed mixture.

6 Pour the mixture into the prepared cake tin and bake in the middle of the oven for 60–70 minutes until golden brown and the cake is coming away from the sides of the tin; a skewer inserted into the centre should come out clean, or with a few moist crumbs clinging to it.

7 Remove from the oven and leave to cool in the tin on a wire rack. Once cool, take the cake out of the tin and remove the baking parchment. The cake can be stored in an airtight container for up to 3 days.

SPICED APPLE CAKE

SERVES 8

185g butter, softened,
  plus extra to grease
3 medium Bramley apples,
  about 700g
1 lemon
185g caster sugar
2 eggs, at room temperature

1 tbsp milk
225g self-raising flour
110g raisins

FOR THE TOPPING
1½ tsp ground cinnamon
25g soft light brown sugar

This delicious cake makes the most of the wonderful flavour of Bramleys. You could also add a handful of blackberries in place of the raisins, in the autumn. You will need a 20cm round cake tin.

1 Heat the oven to 180°C/gas mark 4. Lightly grease the cake tin and line the base with a disc of baking parchment. Peel, core and dice the apples into 1–2cm pieces. Finely grate the lemon zest and squeeze the juice, then stir both into the apple and set aside.

2 Using an electric whisk or wooden spoon, cream the butter and sugar together in a medium bowl until pale, light and fluffy.

3 Break the eggs into a small bowl and beat lightly, using a fork, until broken up. Gradually add the egg to the creamed mixture, in several additions, beating well after each addition. Stir in the milk.

4 Sift the flour over the mixture and scatter over the diced apples and raisins. Sprinkle over the lemon juice and stir until well combined.

5 Pour the mixture into the prepared tin and level off a little with a spoon (it needn't be completely smooth).

6 Mix together the topping ingredients and sprinkle evenly over the top of the cake mixture.

7 Bake in the middle of the oven for 1–1¼ hours until a skewer inserted into the centre of the cake comes out clean, or with only a few moist crumbs clinging to it.

8 Remove from the oven and leave to cool in the tin for a few minutes, before removing to a wire rack to cool. Peel off the baking parchment and serve in slices.

RHUBARB CRUMBLE CAKE

SERVES 8	
85g butter, softened, plus extra to grease	**FOR THE CRUMBLE TOPPING**
85g caster sugar	55g butter
2 small eggs, at room temperature	85g plain flour
85g self-raising flour	30g caster sugar
Pinch of salt	
A little milk, if needed	**TO FINISH**
	Icing sugar, to dust (optional)
FOR THE FILLING	
500g rhubarb	
1 tbsp caster sugar	

The classic pairing of rhubarb and crumble is delicious, and works just as well with cooked apples, apricots or pears in this cake. When rhubarb is out of season, you can use a 400g tin of rhubarb (drained) instead, omitting the sugar. You will need a 20cm round loose-based cake tin.

1 Heat the oven to 190°C/gas mark 5. Lightly grease the tin with a little butter, line the base with a disc of greaseproof paper and grease again (see page 10).

2 Wash and trim the rhubarb and cut it into 1.5–2cm pieces. Set aside.

3 To make the crumble topping, rub the butter into the flour in a small bowl, using your fingertips, until the mixture resembles fine breadcrumbs. Stir in the sugar and set aside.

4 To make the cake, cream the butter and sugar together in a medium bowl, using an electric whisk or a wooden spoon, until pale and fluffy.

5 Break the eggs into a small bowl and beat lightly using a fork. Gradually add the eggs to the creamed mixture, beating well after each addition.

6 Sift over the flour and salt and fold in using a large metal spoon or a spatula. Add 1–2 tbsp milk, if necessary, to achieve a dropping consistency (see page 16).

7 Transfer the mixture to the prepared tin and spread out evenly using a spatula.

8 Toss the rhubarb in the sugar and place carefully and evenly over the cake mixture. Sprinkle the crumble topping over the rhubarb. Bake in the middle of the oven for 60–75 minutes until the top feels firm to the touch.

9 Remove from the oven and leave to cool completely in the tin. Remove from the tin and peel off the lining paper. Dust with icing sugar, if desired, and serve.

APRICOT AND ALMOND UPSIDE DOWN CAKE

SERVES 10

Oil, to grease
500g fresh apricots or
   400g tinned apricot halves
200g apricot jam
170g butter, softened

170g caster sugar
3 eggs, at room temperature
100g self-raising flour
70g ground almonds
1–2 tbsp milk

This is the type of cake that works equally well as a pudding when served straight from the oven. Brush with a little runny honey before serving for an extra shine. You will need a 22cm sandwich tin.

1 Heat the oven to 180°C/gas mark 4. Oil the sandwich tin, line the base with a disc of greaseproof paper and brush lightly with oil again (see page 10). Prepare the fresh apricots, if using, by cutting them through lengthways and removing the stone. If using tinned, drain thoroughly and dry on kitchen paper.

2 Spread the apricot jam over the base of the tin so it is about 5–7mm thick. Place the apricots cut side up in a round circular pattern, in a single layer covering the whole base.

3 In a large bowl, cream the butter and sugar together, using an electric whisk or wooden spoon, until light and fluffy.

4 Break the eggs into a small bowl and beat lightly using a fork to break them up. Add the egg to the creamed mixture in several additions, beating well after each addition until incorporated.

5 Sift the flour and ground almonds over the creamed mixture and fold in. Add enough milk to create a reluctant dropping consistency (see page 16).

6 Scrape the mixture into the prepared tin and smooth over gently. Bake in the middle of the oven for 25–30 minutes until well risen, golden and it feels firm to the touch.

7 Transfer the cake in its tin to a wire rack to cool slightly for about 3 minutes, then turn out onto a serving plate and gently peel away the greaseproof paper. Serve cold, at room temperature or warm, with ice cream or mascarpone.

BLACKBERRY AND APPLE CAKE

SERVES 8–10

Oil, to grease
1 orange
170g butter, softened
170g caster sugar
3 eggs, at room temperature
170g blackberries
170g self-raising flour

FOR THE FILLING
1 large Bramley apple
2 tbsp soft light brown sugar
½ tsp ground cinnamon
4 tbsp water
150ml double cream

TO FINISH
Icing sugar, to dust

This is a lovely way to enjoy the best of these popular autumnal fruits. You will need two 20cm sandwich tins.

1 Heat the oven to 180°C/gas mark 4. Brush the tins with a little oil, line each base with a disc of greaseproof paper and oil again (see page 10). Finely grate the orange zest and set aside.

2 In a large bowl, cream the butter, sugar and orange zest until light and fluffy, using an electric whisk or a wooden spoon. Break the eggs into a small bowl and, using a fork, beat lightly to break them up, then gradually add to the creamed mixture, beating well after each addition. Stir in the blackberries.

3 Sift over the flour and fold it in carefully, using a metal spoon or a spatula and trying not to break up the berries too much. Add a little water to bring the mixture to dropping consistency (see page 16), if necessary.

4 Divide the mixture between the prepared tins and smooth the tops with a spatula. Bake in the middle of the oven for 20–25 minutes, or until well risen, golden and the top springs when pressed lightly with a fingertip.

5 Meanwhile, to make the filling, peel and core the apple, then cut into 1–2cm chunks. Put in a small pan with the sugar, cinnamon and water, cover and cook over a gentle heat until soft. Mash roughly with a fork, then leave to cool.

6 Allow the cakes to cool for a few minutes in the tins, then turn out onto a wire rack. Peel off the lining paper and invert the cakes to right-side up.

7 Lightly whip the cream until it holds its shape, then fold in the cooled apple. Sandwich the cooled cakes together with the apple filling, dust with icing sugar and serve.

TURKISH FIG CAKE
WITH POMEGRANATE SYRUP

SERVES 8–10

170g unsalted butter,
 softened, plus extra
 to grease
Demerara sugar, to sprinkle
4 large, ripe, black figs
140g soft light brown sugar
3 eggs, at room temperature
200g self-raising flour
A pinch of salt
1 tsp baking powder
1½ tsp ground mixed spice

FOR THE FIG PURÉE
200g soft, dried figs
2 tbsp date syrup
3 tbsp water
80ml evaporated milk

**FOR THE POMEGRANATE
SYRUP**
3 tbsp pomegranate molasses
1 tbsp icing sugar
A little boiling water

This cake is absolutely delicious served warm with a spoonful of Greek yoghurt or crème fraîche. The fresh figs, shiny with pomegranate syrup, transform it into a very attractive pudding. You will need a 20cm round loose-based cake tin.

1 Grease the base and sides of the cake tin and sprinkle generously with demerara sugar. Ensure that the tin is evenly coated with the sugar, before lightly tapping out any excess. Cut the fresh figs vertically into quarters, put on a plate, cover with cling film and set aside.

2 To make the fig purée, cut the dried figs into small pieces and put three quarters into a small saucepan with the date syrup and water. Slowly bring to the boil over a medium heat, then reduce the heat and simmer very gently for about 10 minutes, until soft and very pulpy, and all the liquid has been absorbed; the mixture should be quite thick. Spoon into the small bowl of a food processor and process to a purée, or mash well with the back of a wooden spoon. Add the remaining chopped fresh figs to the purée, stir in the evaporated milk and set aside.

3 To make the pomegranate syrup, put the pomegranate molasses and icing sugar in a small bowl. Stir in 1 tbsp boiling water from the kettle and, using a teaspoon, mix together until the icing sugar has dissolved, then set aside. Heat the oven to 180°C/gas mark 4.

4 In a medium bowl, beat the butter and soft light brown sugar, using an electric whisk or wooden spoon, until pale and fluffy. Break the eggs into a small bowl and, using a fork, beat lightly to break them up. Add the eggs to the creamed mixture in several additions, beating well between each one; it should take about 5–6 additions to thoroughly incorporate the eggs.

5 Fold in the fig purée using a large metal spoon or a spatula. Sift the flour into the bowl with the salt, baking powder and mixed spice and fold in carefully, taking care not to beat any of the air out of the mixture.

6 Spoon the mixture into the prepared tin and gently level the top with the back of the spoon. Arrange the cut figs in a decorative pattern on top of the cake, lightly pressing them into the mixture.

7 Bake in the middle of the oven for 50–60 minutes, or until the cake is well risen and golden brown, and a skewer inserted into the centre comes out clean or with just a few moist crumbs clinging to it.

8 Remove from the oven and, using a pastry brush, brush about half of the pomegranate syrup over the cake. Leave to cool in the tin for 10 minutes, then transfer to a wire rack and leave until warm or completely cooled. Brush the cake with the remaining syrup shortly before serving.

GLUTEN-FREE MADEIRA CAKE

160g unsalted butter, softened, plus extra to grease
1 lemon
2 large eggs, at room temperature
130g golden caster sugar, plus 1 tbsp for the top

80g gluten-free plain flour (we find Doves Farm reliable)
1 tsp gluten-free baking powder
Pinch of salt
130g ground almonds

This loaf will keep moist for a few days wrapped in baking parchment and foil and stored in an airtight container. It was extremely popular with our tasters, many of whom could not tell this was a gluten-free cake at all. You will need a 450–500g loaf tin.

1 Heat the oven to 170°C/gas mark 3. Grease the loaf tin, then line the base and short sides with a piece of greaseproof paper that extends over the sides (see page 11).

2 Finely grate the lemon zest and squeeze the juice. Break the eggs into a small bowl and, using a fork, beat lightly to break them up.

3 In a medium bowl, cream the butter and 130g sugar together until pale and fluffy, using an electric whisk. Add the lemon zest and gradually beat in the eggs, beating well after each addition.

4 Sift the flour, baking powder and salt onto the creamed mixture and fold it in gently using a large metal spoon or a spatula, folding in the ground almonds once most of the flour has been incorporated.

5 Add the lemon juice and stir carefully to combine and loosen the mixture.

6 Spoon the mixture into the prepared tin, smooth the surface with a spatula and sprinkle over the 1 tbsp sugar. Bake in the middle of the oven for about 1 hour until a skewer inserted into the centre comes out clean, or with only a few moist crumbs clinging to it. Transfer to a wire rack and leave to cool in the tin.

BRANDIED CHERRY AND MARZIPAN POLENTA CAKE

SERVES 10–12

100g dried cherries
30ml brandy
120g white marzipan
Oil or butter, to grease
120g butter, softened
120g caster sugar

2 eggs, at room temperature
¼ tsp vanilla extract
60g fine polenta
50g plain flour
¼ tsp ground mixed spice
¾ tsp baking powder

This cake would make a great alternative Christmas cake for those who love marzipan but don't like a dense traditional fruit cake. It keeps for up to a week, well wrapped and stored in an airtight container. You need to start this cake a day in advance, to freeze the marzipan and soak the cherries. You will need an 18cm round loose-based cake tin, 5cm deep.

1 Put the dried cherries in a small bowl, pour the brandy over them and then enough boiling water from the kettle to almost cover them. Cover tightly with cling film or a lid and leave to soak overnight. Cut the marzipan into 1–2cm squares and freeze overnight.

2 Heat the oven to 180°C/gas mark 4. Grease and line the cake tin with greaseproof paper (see page 12).

3 Cream the butter and sugar together in a large bowl, using an electric whisk, until pale, light and fluffy.

4 Break the eggs into a small bowl and add the vanilla. Beat lightly with a fork until the eggs are broken up. Gradually add the egg in several additions to the creamed mixture, beating well after each addition.

5 In a separate bowl, sift together the polenta, flour, spice and baking powder, adding any polenta left in the sieve.

6 Fold the dry ingredients into the creamed mixture using a large metal spoon or a spatula, taking care not to over-mix. Drain any liquid from the cherries. Stir three quarters of the cherries and three quarters of the frozen marzipan into the cake mixture, then pour the mixture into the prepared tin. Smooth the top with a spatula.

7 Sprinkle the remaining cherries and marzipan over the top of the cake and push them down slightly with your finger.

8 Bake in the middle of the oven for about 40 minutes, or until well risen, golden and spongy to the touch. Cover with a piece of foil if the cake browns before the centre is cooked. Test with a skewer, but be aware that the melted marzipan can look like uncooked cake mixture, so check carefully in several places.

9 Remove from the oven and leave for a few minutes in the tin, then turn the cake out onto a wire rack to cool a little before peeling off the greaseproof paper (the marzipan will stick to the paper once it is cool). Leave to cool completely before slicing to serve.

BAKEWELL SPONGE CAKE

SERVES 8–10

Oil, to grease
100g white marzipan
4 eggs, at room temperature
110g unsalted butter,
  softened
225g caster sugar
½–1 tsp bitter almond
  extract, to taste
170g self-raising flour
50g flaked almonds

FOR THE RASPBERRY PURÉE
300g fresh raspberries
2 tbsp Framboise syrup

TO FINISH
Icing sugar, to dust

Here all the lovely flavours of a Bakewell sponge pudding come together as a cake. If you don't like marzipan, leave it out altogether, and replace the almond extract with a few drops of vanilla extract to create a raspberry ripple sponge instead. You will need a 23cm round loose-based cake tin.

1 To make the purée, bring the raspberries and Framboise syrup to the boil in a small saucepan over a low heat. Bubble vigorously for 4–6 minutes, stirring occasionally, until the mixture looks quite thick and 'jammy'. Pass through a sieve into a bowl while still hot, and leave to cool completely.

2 Meanwhile, to make the sponge, grease the cake tin and line the base with a disc of baking parchment. Heat the oven to 180°C/gas mark 4.

3 Cut the marzipan into 1.5cm dice and set aside. Break the eggs into a small bowl and, using a fork, beat lightly to break them up.

4 Cream the butter and sugar in a medium bowl, using an electric whisk, until pale, light and fluffy. Add the eggs to the creamed butter and sugar in several additions, beating well between each one (5 or 6 additions will do).

5 Add the almond extract and diced marzipan, folding them into the mixture using a large metal spoon or a spatula. Sift the flour into the bowl and carefully fold it in, trying not to beat any air out of the mixture.

6 Drizzle the cooled raspberry purée over the sponge mixture and fold it in quickly and very lightly, so that it creates a marbled effect; do not be tempted to over-mix, or you will lose the rippled appearance in the cooked cake.

7 Pour the mixture into the prepared cake tin and level it out with the back of the spoon. Sprinkle the flaked almonds over the surface and lightly press them into the mixture using your fingertips.

8 Bake in the middle of the oven for about 50–60 minutes, or until well risen, golden brown and a skewer inserted into the centre comes out clean, or with just a few moist crumbs clinging to it.

9 Remove from the oven and leave the cake to cool in the tin for 10–15 minutes before turning it out onto a wire rack. Peel off the lining paper and leave to cool completely. Before serving, dust generously with icing sugar.

LEMON MERINGUE CAKE

SERVES 8–10

Oil, to grease
1 lemon
225g butter, softened
225g caster sugar
4 eggs, at room temperature
225g self-raising flour
1–2 tbsp milk

FOR THE LEMON CURD
2 lemons
120g caster sugar
50g unsalted butter
2 eggs

FOR THE MERINGUE
2 egg whites, about 60g
110g caster sugar

. . . .

This cake has a soft meringue icing that can be piped or simply swirled on top of the cake, as you choose. Either make the lemon curd in advance, or use a good quality bought one in its place. Any leftover curd can be stored in the fridge and eaten on toast or served with scones in place of jam. You will need two 20cm sandwich tins.

1 To make the lemon curd, finely grate the zest of both lemons and squeeze the juice. Put the juice in a saucepan with the sugar and butter. Beat the eggs in a small bowl with a fork to break them up and add them to the pan.

2 Stir the mixture over a low to medium heat, using a wooden spoon, until the butter and sugar have melted, then increase the heat until the curd just starts to bubble. Remove from the heat and strain through a sieve. Stir in the lemon zest and cover with cling film, so that it touches the surface of the curd to prevent a skin from forming. The curd will thicken as it cools.

3 Heat the oven to 180°C/gas mark 4. Lightly oil the 2 sandwich tins, line the base of each with a disc of greaseproof paper, then lightly brush with oil again (see page 10). Finely grate the lemon zest.

4 Using an electric whisk, cream the butter and sugar together in a medium bowl until pale, light and fluffy.

5 Break the eggs into a separate bowl and beat lightly with a fork. Gradually add the eggs to the creamed mixture in small additions, beating well after each addition.

6 Sift the flour over the creamed mixture and add the lemon zest. Fold in the dry ingredients, using a large metal spoon or a spatula, until the mixture is just combined. Add enough milk to create a reluctant dropping consistency (see page 16).

7 Divide the mixture between the prepared tins, smooth the tops and bake in the middle of the oven for 20–30 minutes, or until well risen, golden and evenly set. The cakes should feel spongy to the touch. Leave them in the tins on a wire rack for a few minutes, then turn out onto the wire rack, peel off the greaseproof paper and leave to cool completely.

8 To make the meringue, put the egg whites into a clean, medium bowl and whisk to stiff peaks (see page 9), using an electric whisk. Add 1 tbsp of the sugar and continue to whisk for 10 seconds, then add a second 1 tbsp sugar and whisk to stiff peaks again. Slowly pour in the remaining sugar, whisking at the same time until it is all incorporated and the meringue is stiff again.

9 Heat the grill to its highest setting, unless you have a cook's blowtorch. Sandwich the 2 cooled sponges together with the cold lemon curd (you may not need to use it all). Decorate the top of the cake with the meringue, either piping it or swirling it over the surface with a palette knife. Avoid creating high peaks, which may burn.

10 To finish, either use a cook's blowtorch (following the manufacturer's instructions) to carefully caramelise the top of the meringue to a golden colour, or place under the hot grill until the top browns, watching carefully as it will burn quickly.

SOMERSET APPLE BRANDY FRUIT CAKE

SERVES 10–12

400g mixed dried fruit
100g dried apples
100g raisins or sultanas
125g butter, softened,
   plus extra to grease
125g soft dark brown sugar
50ml water
50ml orange juice
1 lemon (for zesting
   and juice)
1 orange (for zesting
   and juice)
50ml Somerset cider brandy
¼ tsp freshly grated nutmeg
½ tsp ground cinnamon
½ tsp ground allspice

¼ tsp ground ginger
Pinch of ground cardamom
3 small eggs, at room
   temperature
½ tbsp black treacle
150g plain flour
½ tsp baking powder

TO DECORATE

1 quantity apricot glaze
   (see page 44)
1 tbsp water
250g mixed dried fruit and
   nuts, such as pecans,
   brazils, almonds, apricots,
   peaches, pears, etc.

This cake benefits from being started at least 24 hours, but ideally 3 days, before it is cooked, to make it really moist. For a full flavour, choose a good mixture of dried fruit for the cake, such as dried apricots, peaches, dates, figs, pears, prunes, glacé cherries and mixed peel. You will need a 25cm round cake tin.

1 Dice the mixed dried fruit and dried apples and put in a large saucepan with the raisins, butter, sugar, water and orange juice.

2 Finely grate the lemon and orange zest and squeeze the juice of both fruit. Add half of both to the pan. Over a medium heat, bring the mixture to the boil, stirring gently. Turn the heat down to as low as possible, cover and simmer gently for 10 minutes.

3 Remove the pan from the heat and leave to cool a little before adding the brandy and spices. Transfer the mixture to a large bowl, cover and keep it cool (but ideally not refrigerated) for 3 days, giving it a stir each day.

4 The next day, heat the oven to 170°C/gas mark 3. Grease and line the base and sides of the cake tin with greaseproof paper and grease again (see page 12).

5 Using a wooden spoon, beat the eggs and treacle together in a small bowl, then gradually beat this egg mixture into the soaked fruit mixture.

6 Sift the flour and baking powder onto the mixture and fold in well using a large metal spoon or a spatula. The mixture will be quite loose.

7 Pour the mixture into the prepared tin and bake for about 2–2¼ hours, or until a skewer inserted into the centre comes out clean, or with moist crumbs but no raw mixture attached.

8 Leave the cake to cool in the tin, then remove, wrap well in the lining paper and keep it cool until you are ready to serve it.

9 To decorate the cake, bring the apricot glaze and water to the boil in a small saucepan, then sieve into a bowl. Brush generously over the top of the cake (this will act as the glue). Arrange the fruit and nuts all over the top of the cake, covering as much of the surface as possible, then brush the remaining jam over the surface to glaze it. Tie a ribbon around the cake to decorate. The cake will last for up to 3 months if wrapped carefully in foil and stored in a cool place, but decorate it only when you are ready to serve it.

COVERING A FRUIT CAKE WITH MARZIPAN

Lightly dust a clean surface with icing sugar and roll out the marzipan to a circle, about 20cm in diameter, ensuring the marzipan is moving on the surface and not stuck, and there are as few cracks as possible around the edge. If the cake is not level, shave a little off the top.

1 If the cake is still slightly domed, shape a little marzipan into a thin rope. Secure this around the edge of the cake with a little apricot glaze (to ensure the cake is flat, when turned upside down). Turn the cake upside down and lightly brush the surface (originally the base) and sides with 2–3 tbsp apricot glaze.

To make an apricot glaze...

✳ Put 250g apricot jam (not whole fruit) into a small saucepan with a finely pared strip or two of lemon zest and heat gently, without stirring, until the jam has melted, without letting it boil. If the jam is very thick add 2–3 tbsp warm water to loosen it, then pass through a fine sieve into a bowl, discarding the zest.

2 Place the cake, glazed surface down, in the centre of the marzipan circle and, using your hands, carefully bring the marzipan up against the sides of the cake. Now carefully turn the cake over.

3 Roll lightly across the top of the cake and coax the marzipan down the sides with your hands to the bottom. Roll a jam jar or tin around the sides of the cake, to neaten and smooth the marzipan, ensuring the sides are straight and edges square. Trim to neaten, if necessary. Place on a suitably sized cake board and leave uncovered for about 3 days for the marzipan to dry out. This prevents the almond oils from staining the icing.

TECHNIQUE
COVERING A FRUIT CAKE WITH READY-MADE FONDANT

For an easy way to ice a celebration cake, you can buy ready-made fondant icing or sugar paste, in a block or ready-rolled form. It gives a good finish, but doesn't have the same flavour as traditional royal icing. The marzipan-covered cake must be allowed to dry thoroughly for 3 days before fondant icing is applied.

1 On a work surface lightly dusted with icing sugar, roll out the fondant icing to a thickness of about 3–4mm. Carefully lift the icing onto a rolling pin and lay it over the cake.

2 Smooth the fondant icing over the top surface of the cake and then down the sides, making sure you don't create any pleats or folds.

3 Trim off the excess icing with a knife and neaten the bottom edge against the cake board, tucking the end towards the cake if necessary.

2

WHISKED CAKES

Whisked sponges – made by whisking eggs and sugar together to a mousse-like texture and folding in the flour – are incredibly light and versatile. Their delicate flavour and texture pair well with both subtle and bold flavourings. Genoise – the classic butter-enriched whisked sponge can be layered with delicious fillings, icings and fruits to great effect, which is why it forms the basis of many famous gâteaux.

The only raising agent in a classic whisked cake is the air trapped in tiny bubbles, created when the mixture is whisked to a mousse-like foam. So the most important skills to focus on are whisking the mixture sufficiently 'to the ribbon' (see page 50) and folding in the other ingredients with a minimum of damage to the fragile foam. Using a large metal spoon, and developing a decisive, efficient folding method can help. Also remember to pour the mixture into the tin from as low down as possible, as lots of bubbles are destroyed if you pour from a height.

WHISKED SPONGE

SERVES 8

Oil, to grease
85g caster sugar,
   plus extra to dust
85g plain flour,
   plus extra to dust
Pinch of salt
3 eggs, at room temperature
1½ tbsp warm water

TO ASSEMBLE
200ml whipping cream and
   250g raspberries or
   halved strawberries
OR
½ quantity buttercream
   (see page 152) and
4–5 tbsp raspberry jam

This fatless sponge is best eaten the day it is baked. You will need a 20cm round cake tin.

1 Heat the oven to 180°C/gas mark 4. Oil and line the cake tin and dust with sugar, then flour (see page 11). Sift the flour and salt onto a sheet of greaseproof paper.

2 Put the eggs and sugar in a large heatproof bowl. Using a hand-held electric whisk, start whisking on a low speed without moving the whisk through the mixture until they are combined.

3 Place the bowl over a saucepan of just-boiled water, making sure the bowl is not touching the water. Continue to whisk the mixture on a low speed for 3–4 minutes. This creates a network of small air bubbles, which helps to stabilise the mixture.

4 Increase the speed and continue whisking until the mixture becomes very pale, fluffy and mousse-like, and is 'to the ribbon', holding about a 5–6 second ribbon (see right). Remove the bowl from the pan and continue whisking until the bowl has cooled slightly, a further 1–2 minutes. Lastly, whisk in the water.

5 Sift the flour and salt again over the whisked mixture and, using a large metal spoon, carefully fold it into the mixture.

6 Gently pour the mixture into the prepared tin, holding the bowl as close to the tin as possible, to ensure minimal air loss. Give the tin a little tap on the work surface to bring any large air bubbles to the surface.

7 Stand the cake tin on a baking sheet and bake in the middle of the oven for about 30 minutes. After 25 minutes, you should

be able to smell the sponge. At this point (not before, or the sponge may sink), open the oven door a little and have a look. The sponge should be risen, golden, slightly shrinking away from the sides and crinkly at the edges. When lightly pressed with your fingertips, it should bounce back and not leave an indentation. You may hear a slight creaking when you press it.

8 Stand the sponge, still in its tin, on a wire rack to cool a little for 1–2 minutes, then carefully invert it and leave upside down on the wire rack, still in the tin, to cool completely.

9 To release the sponge from the tin, run a cutlery knife around the side of the sponge, keeping the knife against the tin. Once the sponge is fully released, carefully turn it onto a clean hand and gently place back on the wire rack. Peel off the lining paper.

10 To serve, cut the cake horizontally into 2 even layers and sandwich together with whipped cream and fresh berries or buttercream and jam.

A note on 'to the ribbon'...

✳ When the beaters are lifted, the mixture should fall from them onto the surface of the mixture in a wide ribbon-like trail and hold itself there for a few seconds before sinking in (as shown in step 4). When a recipe calls for a 4 or 5 or 6 second ribbon, this refers to the length of time the ribbon trail holds. Normally a 5–6 second ribbon is required, but check the recipe.

1 Shaking the excess flour out of the prepared cake tin.

2 Whisking the eggs and sugar together on a low speed to combine.

3 Whisking the mixture over hot water to encourage it to thicken and increase in volume.

4 Checking that the mixture has reached the correct 'to the ribbon' stage.

(Continued overleaf)

5 Carefully folding in the flour, using a large metal spoon, to avoid beating out any air that has been incorporated during whisking.

6 Gently pouring the mixture into the prepared cake tin.

7 Pressing the sponge very lightly with the fingertips to test whether it is ready. There should be a spongy set all over the surface and the cake should have shrunk slightly away from the sides of the tin.

8 Inverting the cooked sponge onto the wire rack to cool.

LEMON AND MACADEMIA CAKE

120g macademia nuts
Butter, to grease
3 large eggs, at room
    temperature
2 lemons

50g self-raising flour
100g caster sugar
Drop of vanilla extract
160g icing sugar

This is a very decadent take on the humble lemon drizzle cake, and is great for special occasions. You will need a 450–500g loaf tin.

1 Heat the oven to 180°C/gas mark 4. Spread the macademia nuts out on a baking sheet and bake for 8–10 minutes until lightly golden. Tip onto a plate and set aside to cool.

2 Meanwhile, lightly grease the loaf tin, then line the base and short sides with a strip of baking parchment that extends over the sides (see page 11). Separate the eggs into 2 medium bowls (see page 8). Finely grate the zest of the lemons and squeeze the juice. Set aside.

3 Transfer 100g of the cooled nuts to the small bowl of a food processor and add the flour and 2 tbsp of the sugar. Process briefly until the nuts are broken down to the consistency of nibbed almonds, taking care not to over-grind them or they will release oil that will interfere with the meringue. Roughly chop the remaining nuts and reserve for decoration.

4 Set aside another 2 tbsp of the sugar, then add the remaining sugar, lemon zest and vanilla to the yolks and beat, using an electric whisk, until the mixture increases in volume and becomes pale and mousse-like. Set aside.

5 Using a clean whisk, whisk the egg whites to stiff peaks (see page 9), then add the reserved sugar and continue to whisk for about 20 seconds, or until the mixture returns to stiff peaks.

6 Carefully fold the ground nuts and flour into the yolk mixture. Now stir in a spoonful of the whisked whites to loosen the mixture. Add the remaining whites and, using a spatula or large metal spoon, carefully fold the mixtures together until evenly combined. Do not over-fold or the mixture will lose volume.

7 Working quickly, gently pour the mixture into the prepared loaf tin, holding the bowl as close to the tin as possible to ensure minimal air loss. Cook in the middle of the oven for 30–40 minutes until well risen and lightly golden. Test by inserting a skewer into the centre of the cake; it should come out with a few moist crumbs clinging to it, but no raw mixture.

8 Leave the cake to cool in the tin for 10 minutes before carefully turning out onto a wire rack to cool completely. Remove the lining paper once cooled.

9 Meanwhile, to make the icing, sift the icing sugar into a bowl and gradually add the lemon juice, stirring well until smooth. If the mixture seems too thick, beat in a few drops of water to achieve a slightly runnier consistency.

10 When the cake is cool, carefully drizzle the lemon icing over the top, allowing it to run down the sides a little. Sprinkle the reserved chopped nuts onto the icing and leave the cake to stand for 15 minutes to allow the icing to set. Cut into slices to serve.

CLASSIC SWISS ROLL

SERVES 8–10

Oil, to grease
85g caster sugar,
    plus extra to dust
85g plain flour,
    plus extra to dust
Pinch of salt

3 eggs, at room temperature
2–3 drops of vanilla extract
1½ tbsp warm water

TO ASSEMBLE
5–6 tbsp raspberry jam

This classic teatime favourite is made using a whisked sponge mixture and is best eaten on the day it is made. Once rolled, store in an airtight container, wrapped in its paper to prevent it from drying out, until ready to serve. You will need a 30 x 20cm Swiss roll tin.

1 Line the Swiss roll tin with baking parchment or prepare a paper case: cut 2 sheets of baking parchment to a size 2cm bigger all around than an A4 sheet of paper. Fold up a 2cm edge on each side and fold and clip the corners with paper clips. Place this on a baking sheet.

2 Prepare the whisked sponge mixture (following the method on page 50), adding the vanilla extract after whisking the eggs and sugar together. Spread the mixture into the prepared tin or paper case, smoothing it to the edges gently, to avoid knocking out the air. Bake for just 12–15 minutes.

3 While the cooked sponge is still warm, lay a piece of greaseproof paper on the work surface and sprinkle it evenly with caster sugar. Invert the warm sponge onto the sugared paper and carefully peel off the paper, using a palette knife to support the cake. Trim off the dry edges.

4 Make a shallow cut across the width of the cake; this helps to get a well shaped roll. While the sponge is still warm, spread it with 5–6 tbsp raspberry jam. Using the paper under the cake to help, roll the cake up firmly and evenly from the cut end. Leave the Swiss roll wrapped in the paper to set its shape.

5 When ready to serve, carefully unroll the paper, then dredge the Swiss roll with a little more caster sugar.

6 Using a serrated knife, cut the Swiss roll into even slices.

BUTTERSCOTCH AND ALMOND SWISS ROLL

SERVES 10

110g plain flour
1 tsp baking powder
Pinch of salt
200g caster sugar
120ml sunflower oil
4 egg yolks and 6 egg whites,
    at room temperature
60ml water
1 tsp vanilla extract
¼ tsp cream of tartar

FOR THE BUTTERSCOTCH SAUCE
85g unsalted butter
210g dark brown sugar
225ml double cream
1½ tsp vanilla extract

FOR THE FILLING
60g slivered almonds
350ml double cream

Oozing with cream and butterscotch, this cake is sheer decadence. You will need a 42 x 30cm Swiss roll tin.

1 To make the butterscotch sauce, melt the butter in a large saucepan over a medium heat. Stir in the brown sugar, then bring to a simmer and cook, stirring often, until the sugar melts and the mixture begins to thicken, about 3 minutes. Stir in a quarter of the cream to combine, then add the remaining cream and bring to the boil, stirring occasionally, until it has darkened, about 8–10 minutes. Remove from the heat, leave to cool slightly, then stir in the vanilla. Set aside to cool completely.

2 Heat the oven to 180°C/gas mark 4. Line the Swiss roll tin with baking parchment (see page 56).

3 Sift the flour, baking powder, salt and 90g of the caster sugar into a large bowl. In a small bowl, whisk together the oil, egg yolks, water and vanilla. Add the liquid mixture to the dry ingredients and stir quickly, until smooth and batter-like.

4 In a clean bowl, whisk the egg whites, using an electric whisk on medium speed, until frothy. Add the cream of tartar, increase the speed to high and whisk until the whites begin to form stiff peaks. Reduce to medium speed and gradually add the remaining caster sugar, then increase to high and continue whisking until the whites form stiff, shiny peaks. Using a large spoon or a spatula, fold one third of the whites into the batter, then carefully fold in the remaining whites until just combined.

5 Pour the mixture into the prepared tin and smooth the surface gently, using a spatula. Bake in the middle of the oven for 15–20 minutes, or until the sponge is golden and it springs back when lightly touched with the fingertips.

6 Remove from the oven and slide the cake and parchment out of the tin onto a wire rack. Cover with a slightly damp tea towel to prevent the cake from cracking and leave to cool completely. Increase the oven temperature to 190°C/gas mark 5.

7 Meanwhile, for the filling, scatter the almonds onto a baking tray and toast in the oven, tossing occasionally, until just golden brown, about 10 minutes. Tip onto a plate and set aside to cool.

8 Half-fill a large bowl with cold water and a handful of ice cubes and place a slightly smaller bowl inside. Add the cream and 225ml of the butterscotch sauce to the smaller bowl and, using an electric whisk, whisk on a medium speed until blended. Increase the speed and whisk to soft peaks that just hold their shape, taking care not to over-whisk or it will curdle.

9 To assemble the Swiss roll, place a piece of baking parchment just larger than the cake on a clean work surface. Remove the damp tea towel, quickly turn the cake over onto the paper and peel away the parchment. Spread half the butterscotch cream evenly over the cake and sprinkle with three quarters of the toasted almonds.

10 Roll up the Swiss roll (see page 57), removing the paper as you go. Place on a serving dish and coat with the remaining butterscotch cream, smoothing it with a palette knife. Sprinkle with the reserved almonds. Just before serving, warm the rest of the butterscotch sauce. Drizzle over individual slices to serve.

TECHNIQUE
WHISKING CREAM

When cream is whisked, air bubbles are trapped, thickening and lightening the cream so it can be used for cake fillings and toppings. It is all too easy to over-whisk cream. To help avoid the grainy texture of over-whipped cream, make sure the cream is cold before you whisk it. On a hot day, it is a good idea to whisk cream slowly, as it can suddenly thicken.

If you are adding sweetness and flavourings to cream, such as icing or caster sugar, vanilla seeds or grated orange zest, add them before you start whisking; if added at the end over-whisking is more likely.

If you are folding whipped cream into a sweet cake filling, taste it when the other ingredients have been added, then adjust the sweetness accordingly.

SOFT PEAK When whisked to this stage, cream is thick enough to form soft peaks that hold briefly as you lift the whisk, then dissipate back into the cream. If cream is to be folded into another mixture, such as crème pâtissière, it should be of a similar consistency, usually soft peak.

MEDIUM PEAK To use for sandwiching cakes together or for piping, cream needs to be whisked to a slightly firmer peak, so it is just holding its shape but not splitting or looking ragged and textured if piped.

PIPING CONSISTENCY When piping whipped cream, it may overheat in a piping bag held by warm hands, and the last of the cream may curdle before it is piped. To avoid this, slightly under-whisk the cream, or only half-fill the piping bag.

GENOISE

SERVES 8

Oil, to grease
125g caster sugar,
    plus extra to dust
125g plain flour,
    plus extra to dust
55g butter
4 eggs, at room temperature

TO ASSEMBLE
1 quantity buttercream
    (see pages 152)
1 quantity praline, crushed
    (see page 153)

A genoise differs from a whisked sponge in that it contains butter, which enriches the cake and also means it will last longer before becoming stale. You will need a 20cm moule à manqué (tin with sloping sides) or round cake tin.

1 Heat the oven to 180°C/gas mark 4. Lightly oil the cake tin and line the base with a disc of greaseproof paper. Lightly oil again. Dust with sugar then flour, tapping out the excess (see page 11).

2 Melt the butter in a small saucepan over a low heat, then set aside to cool.

3 Place the eggs and sugar in a large heatproof bowl and, using a hand-held electric whisk, start whisking on a low speed without moving the whisk through the eggs and sugar. Place the bowl over a saucepan of just boiled water, making sure the base is not touching the water, and continue to whisk on a low speed for 3–4 minutes. Increase the speed and continue whisking until the mixture becomes very pale, fluffy and mousse-like, and holds a 5–6 second ribbon (see page 50).

4 Remove the bowl from the pan and continue whisking until the bowl has cooled slightly, a further 1–2 minutes.

5 Carefully pour the melted, cooled butter around the edge of the mixture and fold it in, using a large metal spoon, with just 3 or 4 folds.

6 Sift the flour over the mixture and carefully fold it in, taking care not to beat any air out of the mixture.

7 Gently spoon the mixture into the prepared tin, holding the bowl as close to the tin as possible to ensure as little air loss as possible. Give the tin a little tap on the work surface to bring any large air bubbles to the surface.

8 Stand the cake tin on a baking sheet. Cook in the middle of the oven for about 30–35 minutes. After 25 minutes, you should be able to smell the sponge. At this point (not before, or the sponge may sink), open the oven door a little and have a look. It should be risen, golden, slightly shrinking away from the sides and crinkly at the edges. When lightly pressed with your fingertips it should bounce back.

9 Stand the sponge, still in its tin, on a wire rack to cool a little for 1–2 minutes, then carefully invert it and leave upside down on the wire rack, still in the tin, to cool completely.

10 To release the sponge from the tin, run a cutlery knife around the side of the sponge, keeping the knife firmly against the tin (as shown on page 53). Once fully released, carefully turn the sponge onto a clean hand and carefully place back down on the wire rack. Peel off the lining paper.

11 To serve, cut the cake horizontally into 2 layers and sandwich together with a third of the buttercream. Spread the remaining buttercream over the top and sides and coat the sides with the crushed praline. Smooth the buttercream top decoratively with a palette knife.

Variations

✻ **Coffee genoise** Dissolve 2–3 tsp good quality instant coffee granules in 2 tsp hot water, let cool and add with the butter.

✻ **Chocolate genoise** Reduce the flour to 85g and add 40g dark cocoa powder.

✻ **Lemon genoise** Fold in the finely grated zest of 1 lemon with the butter.

STEP 5 Pouring the melted, cooled butter around the edge of the mixture.

STEP 5 Carefully folding in the butter, with a large metal spoon, using just 3 or 4 folds to fully incorporate it.

STEP 6 Sifting the flour over the mixture, ready to fold it in carefully.

STEP 7 Gently spooning the mixture into the prepared moulé à manqué tin.

MOJITO GENOISE

FOR THE GENOISE
Oil, to grease
125g caster sugar,
    plus extra to dust
125g plain flour,
    plus extra to dust
55g butter
4 eggs, at room temperature

FOR THE SYRUP
100g sugar
100ml water
70ml rum
70ml lime juice
Large sprig of fresh mint

FOR THE FROSTING
150g salted butter, softened
250g icing sugar
1 tbsp milk
1 lime
1–1½ tbsp rum

TO DECORATE
1 egg white
Handful of small mint sprigs
Caster sugar, to dust

This is a fabulous new version of a classic – perfect for a decadent celebration. You will need a 20cm moule à manqué (tin with sloping sides) or round cake tin.

1 Heat the oven to 180°C/gas mark 4, lightly oil the cake tin and line the base with a disc of greaseproof paper. Dust with sugar and then flour (see page 11). Make the genoise sponge following the recipe on page 60.

2 To make the syrup, dissolve the sugar in the water in a heavy-based pan, using the handle of a wooden spoon to agitate the sugar so it does not 'cake' on the base of the pan.

3 When all the sugar has dissolved, boil the syrup for 2–3 minutes, then add the rum and lime juice. Lightly bruise the mint, add to the syrup and leave to infuse for 10–15 minutes. Taste and adjust the flavour as necessary: there should be a balance between sugar, lime, rum and mint, with none of the flavours particularly dominant.

4 To make the frosting, beat the butter in a medium bowl with a hand-held electric whisk until smooth. Add half the icing sugar and continue to beat until smooth. Add the remaining icing sugar with the milk and beat until light, creamy and smooth. Finely grate the lime zest and squeeze the juice. Add the rum, lime juice and zest to the frosting, to taste.

5 To assemble, cut the cake in half horizontally (see page 19). Remove the mint from the syrup and, using a teaspoon, drizzle the syrup over both cut sides of the cake, letting it soak in gently. The syrup should moisten and flavour the cake rather than saturate it, so you may not need to use it all.

6 Lightly beat the egg white for the decoration, and use to brush the mint sprigs. Dust with caster sugar and set aside.

7 Use half the frosting to sandwich the 2 cake layers together. Spread the remaining frosting over the top of the cake as evenly as possible and scatter the mint sprigs on top to decorate.

LEMON AND ORANGE FLOWER WATER CAKE

Oil, to grease
1 orange
55g butter
5 eggs, at room temperature
170g caster sugar
½ tbsp orange flower water
170g plain flour
¼ tsp baking powder

TO FINISH
8 tbsp orange curd (or lemon
   curd if orange unavailable)
Icing sugar, to dust

Orange flower water adds a delicate fragrance to this citrus cake. Don't be tempted to add any more to the mixture, as the flavour can become rather medicinal. Alternatively, you can replace it with a couple of drops of orange oil. You will need a 20cm round cake tin.

1 Heat the oven to 180°C/gas mark 4. Lightly oil the tin and line the base with a disc of greaseproof paper.

2 Finely grate the orange zest and squeeze the juice; set aside separately. Melt the butter in a small pan over a low heat, then set aside to cool until tepid.

3 Separate the eggs into 2 large bowls (see page 8) and, using an electric whisk, whisk the yolks with 85g of the caster sugar until pale and fluffy. Whisk in the orange flower water, orange zest and 2 tbsp orange juice.

4 Whisk the egg whites until stiff (see page 9), then gradually whisk in the remaining sugar until very thick and shiny.

5 Sift the flour with the baking powder to combine; set aside.

6 Fold 1 large spoonful of egg whites into the egg yolk mixture, using a large metal spoon or a spatula, then fold in the cooled melted butter. Fold in the remaining egg whites until they have all but disappeared, then sift the flour and baking powder over the surface of the mixture and fold in carefully.

7 Pour into the prepared tin and bake in the middle of the oven for about 25–30 minutes until risen, golden and slightly shrunken away from the sides of the tin. It should spring back when lightly touched on the surface with a fingertip.

8 Remove from the oven and leave to cool a little before carefully loosening the sides of the cake with a knife. Turn out the cake onto a wire rack and leave to cool completely before removing the lining paper.

9 When cold, cut the cake in half horizontally (see page 19), sandwich it together with the curd and dust with icing sugar.

TIRAMISU CAKE

SERVES 8–10

Oil, to grease
125g caster sugar,
   plus extra to dust
100g plain flour,
   plus extra to dust
55g butter
2 tsp instant espresso
   coffee granules
2 tsp boiling water
4 large eggs, at room
   temperature
½ tsp baking powder

FOR THE SYRUP
30g granulated sugar
5 tbsp water
2 tbsp Marsala

FOR THE FILLING
2–3 tbsp Marsala
250g mascarpone or
   cream cheese
2 tsp icing sugar, or to taste

TO FINISH
Cocoa powder, to dust

Here all the flavours of a traditional tiramisu are brought together in an impressive cake. Enjoy a slice with a cup of coffee or serve as a pudding, perhaps with a spoonful of sweetened mascarpone or some chocolate curls. You will need a 20cm round cake tin.

1 Heat the oven to 180°C/gas mark 4. Lightly oil the tin, line the base with a disc of greaseproof paper and oil again. Dust with caster sugar and then with flour, tapping out the excess (see page 11).

2 Melt the butter in a small pan, then set aside to cool until tepid. Dissolve the coffee in the boiling water and set aside.

3 Break the eggs into a heatproof bowl and add the sugar. With a hand-held electric whisk, start whisking on a low speed, then place the bowl over a saucepan of gently simmering water, making sure the base of the bowl is not touching the water. Whisk until the mixture has doubled in bulk, using a hand-held electric whisk. Remove the bowl from the pan, add the coffee and continue whisking, off the heat, until the mixture is cooled.

4 Sift over the flour and baking powder, quickly pour the cooled melted butter around the edge of the bowl and fold in swiftly (if you work too slowly the cake will lose volume).

5 Pour the mixture into the prepared tin and spread it out evenly. Bake in the middle of the oven for 30–35 minutes until the top springs back when pressed lightly with a fingertip.

6 Remove from the oven and leave to cool slightly in the tin, then turn out onto a wire rack and leave to cool completely before removing the lining paper.

7 To make the syrup, put the sugar and water into a heavy-based saucepan and stir over a low heat, without boiling, until the sugar has dissolved completely. Increase the heat, bring to the boil and boil until syrupy. Remove from the heat, allow to cool slightly, then add the Marsala.

8 Split the cooled cake in half horizontally (see page 19), brush the cut halves with the syrup and leave to cool on a wire rack.

9 To make the filling, put the Marsala and mascarpone in a bowl and mix together. Sift in the icing sugar, adding more to taste if needed.

10 Sandwich the cake halves together with the filling and, just before serving, sift a little cocoa powder over the top to finish.

HAZELNUT AND APPLE CAKE

Oil, to grease
110g skinned hazelnuts
110g caster sugar
55g butter
4 eggs, plus 1 extra white,
   at room temperature
100g plain flour

FOR THE FILLING
2 cooking apples,
   about 300g in total
10g butter
Small strip of thinly pared
   lemon zest
3 tbsp Calvados
55–85g soft light
   brown sugar

TO FINISH
Icing sugar, to dust

The apple purée, flavoured with Calvados, makes a tangy filling for this delicious nutty cake. Alternatively, if you prefer a richer filling, whisk 250ml double cream with 1 tbsp icing sugar and 1 tbsp Calvados until it holds its shape and use this in place of the apple filling. You will need a 20cm round cake tin.

1 To make the filling, wash, quarter and core the apples (do not peel), then slice thinly.

2 Melt the butter in a medium pan over a low heat, then add the apples, lemon zest and Calvados. Cover and cook over a gentle heat, stirring occasionally, until completely soft. Push through a sieve into a measuring jug.

3 Return the measured purée to the rinsed out pan and add at least 55g sugar to 600ml purée. Cook rapidly for about 4 minutes until the mixture reaches a dropping consistency (see page 16). Remove from the heat and leave the apple purée to cool completely.

4 Heat the oven to 180°C/gas mark 4. Lightly oil the cake tin and line the base with a disc of greaseproof paper.

5 Spread the hazelnuts out on a baking tray and toast in the oven for 8–10 minutes. Tip onto a plate to cool, then finely grind in a food processor with 1 tbsp of the sugar.

6 Melt the butter in a small pan over a low heat, then remove from the heat and leave to cool until tepid.

7 Separate the whole eggs into 2 bowls (see page 8), adding the extra white to the yolks. Using an electric whisk, whisk the egg yolks and single white with all but 1 tbsp of the remaining sugar, until pale and creamy.

8 Whisk the remaining egg whites until stiff (see page 9), then whisk in the remaining 1 tbsp sugar.

9 Pour the cooled butter around the edge of the egg yolk mixture. Sift over the flour, add the ground hazelnuts and fold in carefully using a large metal spoon or a spatula. Carefully fold in the whisked egg whites.

10 Pile the mixture into the prepared tin and gently smooth the top with a spatula. Bake in the middle of the oven for 40–50 minutes until firm to the touch and just shrinking away from the sides of the tin.

11 Remove from the oven and leave to cool a little in the tin before carefully removing to a wire rack to cool completely. Peel off the lining paper.

12 Cut the cooled cake in half horizontally (see page 19) and sandwich together using the apple filling. Dredge the top of the cake with icing sugar and serve with whipped cream.

CARAMEL GENOISE WITH SALTED CARAMEL FROSTING

SERVES 8–10

FOR THE CARAMEL GENOISE
50g unsalted butter,
    plus extra to grease
150g caster sugar,
    plus extra to dust
110g plain flour,
    plus extra to dust
75ml water
4 eggs, at room temperature

FOR THE SALTED CARAMEL FROSTING
115g granulated sugar
45ml water
115ml double cream
½ tsp vanilla extract
Large pinch of flaked sea salt,
    to taste
265g salted butter, softened
340g icing sugar

When you have mastered the basic genoise, try this delicious version where the base is flavoured with caramel. Make sure all your ingredients are organised and you are familiar with the recipe before you start, as the caramel needs to be used as soon as it is the right colour. You will need a 20–22cm round cake tin.

1 Heat the oven to 180°C/gas mark 4. Put the butter in a small saucepan over a low heat until just melted, then remove from the heat and leave to cool.

2 Lightly grease the cake tin and line the base with a disc of greaseproof paper. Grease again and dust with sugar, then flour (see page 11).

3 To make the caramel, dissolve half the sugar in the water in a small saucepan over a gentle heat. Once all the sugar has dissolved, increase the heat, bring the syrup to the boil, without stirring, and boil until it caramelises to a deep golden colour. (The caramel needs to be ready once the egg and remaining sugar mousse is to a 5–6 second ribbon, see below.)

4 Meanwhile, put the eggs and remaining sugar in a medium heatproof bowl and, using a hand-held electric whisk, start to whisk until combined. Place the bowl over a pan of just-boiled water, making sure the base is not touching the water. Continue whisking on a slow speed to create a stable mousse. Once the mousse is at a 5–6 second ribbon (see page 50), remove the bowl from the pan and pour in the caramel slowly, continuing to whisk until the caramel is fully incorporated.

5 Fold in the cooled melted butter, then sift the flour over the surface and fold it in carefully. Pour the mixture into the prepared tin and bake in the middle of the oven for 25–30 minutes until golden and slightly shrinking from the sides of the tin. When pressed lightly, no indentation should remain.

6 Remove from the oven and stand on a wire rack to cool before carefully removing the cake from the tin and peeling away the lining paper.

7 For the salted caramel frosting, put the sugar and water in a pan and make a caramel (following step 3, left). Once the caramel is a deep golden colour, add the cream and vanilla; the mixture will sputter and spit, so take care. Stir to ensure the caramel is fully dissolved, then remove from the heat and leave to cool. Add the sea salt to taste.

8 Beat the butter and icing sugar together with an electric whisk until light and fluffy, then add the caramel sauce 1 tbsp at a time, beating well after each addition, until smooth and aerated. Taste and add more salt if necessary.

9 Cut the cooled cake in half horizontally through the middle (see page 19). Use half of the icing to sandwich the cake halves together, and the remainder to ice the top of the cake.

BLOOD ORANGE AND OLIVE OIL CAKE

SERVES 8	
Butter, to grease	1 tsp baking powder
190g plain flour,	¼ tsp bicarbonate of soda
plus extra to dust	Pinch of salt
2–3 blood oranges	80g full-fat natural yoghurt
200g caster sugar	2 tbsp granulated sugar
120ml extra virgin olive oil	100g icing sugar
2 eggs, at room temperature	

This cake uses the colour of the blood orange juice to colour the icing, so when the oranges are very deep red, it can be rather a shocking pink. If you prefer a more muted colour use the juice of normal oranges instead. It works well with any tart citrus fruit such as lemon, lime or grapefruit. Just replace the blood orange zest and juice with the fruit of your choice. You will need a 20cm round cake tin.

1 Heat the oven to 180°C/gas mark 4. Lightly grease the cake tin, line the base with a disc of greaseproof paper and grease again. Coat lightly with flour before tapping out the excess (see page 11).

2 Finely grate enough blood orange zest to give you 2 tbsp, and squeeze enough juice to give you 135ml juice; set both aside.

3 In a large bowl, mix together the caster sugar, orange zest and olive oil, then whisk in the eggs one at a time and mix until well combined.

4 In a separate bowl, sift together the flour, baking powder, bicarbonate of soda and salt. Stir the dry ingredients into the sugar and egg mixture.

5 In a small bowl, mix 30ml of the blood orange juice with the yoghurt and stir this into the mixture.

6 Pour the mixture into the prepared tin and gently smooth the top with a spatula. Tap the tin sharply a couple of times on the work surface to release any large air bubbles. Bake in the middle of the oven for 50–60 minutes until a skewer inserted into the centre comes out clean, or with only a few moist crumbs clinging to it.

7 Meanwhile, to make the syrup, simmer 80ml of the blood orange juice with the granulated sugar in a small saucepan over a gentle heat until the sugar dissolves and the syrup thickens a little. Remove from the heat and set aside to cool.

8 Remove the cooked cake from the oven and leave to cool for 10 minutes in the tin before transferring to a wire rack. Using a skewer or a cocktail stick, poke holes evenly over the surface of the cake, down to the centre, then spoon the blood orange syrup over the cake, allowing the cake to cool completely while absorbing the syrup.

9 To make the glaze, sift the icing sugar into a bowl and add the remaining 25ml orange juice, whisking until smooth. Pour over the cooled cake and allow the icing to set before serving.

CHOCOLATE POLENTA CAKE (GLUTEN-FREE)

Oil, to grease
140g caster sugar,
    plus extra to dust
Rice flour, to dust
225g good quality dark
    chocolate (70% cocoa
    solids)

115g unsalted butter
70ml espresso coffee
5 eggs, at room temperature
3 tbsp dark rum
85g fine polenta

The addition of coffee enhances the flavour of the chocolate here, rather than giving the cake a mocha taste. The cake is turned directly onto a serving plate as it is quite fragile and can break if moved around. It has a lovely light texture and is ideal for those who are avoiding gluten. You will need a 22cm round cake tin.

1 Heat the oven to 180°C/gas mark 4. Lightly oil the cake tin, line the base with a disc of greaseproof paper, then brush the disc with oil. Dust with caster sugar and then with a little rice flour, tapping out any excess (see page 11).

2 Cut the chocolate and butter into small pieces and put in a heatproof bowl. Set the bowl over a saucepan of just-boiled water, ensuring the bowl is not touching the water. Give the mixture an occasional stir to encourage it to melt. When almost melted, stir in the espresso and set aside to cool.

3 Separate the eggs, putting the yolks in a medium bowl and the whites in a large bowl (see page 8). Add 85g of the sugar to the yolks along with 1 tbsp of the rum and, using an electric whisk, beat well until pale and thick.

4 With clean beaters, whisk the egg whites to the medium peak stage (see page 9). Gradually whisk in the remaining sugar until the mixture is thick and glossy.

5 Using a large metal spoon or a spatula, fold the melted chocolate mixture into the yolk mixture along with the remaining rum and the polenta. Gently fold in the egg whites.

6 Pour the mixture into the prepared tin and bake in the middle of the oven for 40–50 minutes until a skewer inserted into the centre comes out clean.

7 Remove from the oven and leave the cake to cool in the tin for 10 minutes, then turn out onto a serving plate and remove the lining paper. Leave to cool completely before cutting into slices and serving with crème fraîche.

TORTA NOCE DI COCCO (GLUTEN-FREE)

SERVES 6–8

Oil, to grease
100g good quality dark
    chocolate, 70% cocoa
    solids
6 large eggs, at room
    temperature

125g raw organic coconut oil
250g caster sugar
1 tsp vanilla extract
Good quality cocoa powder,
    to dust

This recipe happens to be gluten- and dairy-free, and uses coconut oil, which is being used more and more in home baking for its subtle coconut flavour as much as for its associated health benefits. Coconut oil should be kept in a cool, dark place but not the fridge. It is solid when cool, and needs to be brought to warm room temperature before using. This cake is delicious served with crème fraîche, or dairy-free ice cream. You will need a 23cm round springform cake tin.

1 Heat the oven to 170°C/gas mark 3. Lightly oil the cake tin, line the base with a disc of greaseproof and lightly oil the disc.

2 Cut the chocolate into small pieces and put in a heatproof bowl. Set the bowl over a saucepan of just-boiled water, ensuring the bowl is not touching the water. Give the chocolate an occasional stir to encourage it to melt. Once melted, remove the bowl from the pan.

3 Separate the eggs, putting the yolks in a medium bowl and the whites in a large bowl (see page 8). Add the coconut oil, sugar and vanilla to the yolks and stir well, then mix in the melted chocolate.

4 Using a hand-held electric whisk, whisk the egg whites to medium peaks (see page 9), then fold them carefully into the cake mixture, using a large metal spoon or a spatula.

5 Pour the mixture into the prepared cake tin and bake for 1 hour, checking after 45 minutes by inserting a skewer into the centre. If the centre is very liquid, leave for the full hour.

6 Remove from the oven and carefully release the edge of the cake from the tin, using a sharp, thin-bladed knife. Leave to cool in the tin.

7 Just before serving, carefully remove the cake from the tin and remove the lining paper. Sift some cocoa powder over the surface of the cake.

3

ALL-IN-ONE QUICK CAKES

This is the chapter to turn to when you have no time to bake!
The basic quantities of butter, sugar, flour and eggs are the
same as for creamed cakes, but as the title suggests, the
ingredients are all beaten together, making these very quick
and easy cakes to produce. They will generally be a little
denser than their creamed equivalents, but all-in-one cakes
are a great way of turning out a delicious cake with the
minimum amount of time and effort.

LIME DRIZZLE CAKE

SERVES 6–8

100g butter, softened plus extra to grease	125g self-raising flour
2 limes	1 scant tsp baking powder
2 eggs	100g caster sugar
2 tbsp milk	50g granulated sugar

This is an easy adaptation of the creaming method in which all the ingredients are beaten together at the same time, which gives surprisingly good results. You will need a 450–500g loaf tin.

1 Heat the oven to 170°C/gas mark 3. Grease the loaf tin, then line the base and short sides with a piece of greaseproof paper that extends over the sides (see page 11).

2 Finely grate the lime zest and squeeze the juice. Beat the eggs and milk together in a small bowl.

3 Sift the flour and baking powder into a large bowl and stir in the caster sugar. Cut the butter into small cubes and add to the bowl. Add the egg mixture and lime zest and beat with an electric whisk until smooth, about 1 minute. The mixture should have a dropping consistency (see page 16).

4 Pour the mixture into the prepared loaf tin and bake for 35–40 minutes, or until the top springs back when pressed lightly. Test by inserting a skewer into the centre; it should come out with a few moist crumbs but no raw mixture.

5 Leave to cool in the tin for 5 minutes before turning it out onto a wire rack to cool a little more. Meanwhile, put the granulated sugar in a small bowl and stir in enough lime juice to make a runny syrup.

6 Return the cake to the tin while still a little warm and pour the syrup over the loaf. Leave to cool completely, then remove the cake from the tin by lifting the greaseproof paper ends. Cut into slices to serve.

Variation

✻ **Lemon drizzle cake** Use 1 large lemon in place of the limes.

A note on softened butter...

✻ To soften butter for making all-in-one or creamed cakes, it is best to leave the butter out of the fridge overnight to ensure it is evenly softened throughout. If this isn't possible, take it out of the fridge at least 2 hours in advance and leave in a warm part of the kitchen (but not on the stove as it will become greasy if it starts to melt). Alternatively, use the microwave in 10 second blasts, allowing it to stand for several minutes and changing its position in between blasts or the centre will melt.

CARROT CAKE

SERVES 10–12

370g sunflower oil, plus
  extra to grease
250–300g carrots
120g walnuts, plus a few
  extra to decorate
250g plain flour
2 tsp bicarbonate of soda
1 tsp salt
2 tsp ground mixed spice
2 tsp ground cinnamon
4 eggs

165g soft light brown sugar
290g granulated sugar
135g tinned crushed
  pineapple (drained weight)

FOR THE ICING
1 lemon
190g icing sugar
105g cream cheese
90g butter, softened

This is the ultimate carrot cake, standing almost as tall as it is round. Don't be put off by the long cooking time. It is worth the wait. You will need a 20cm springform round cake tin.

1 Heat the oven to 150°C/gas mark 2. Lightly oil the base and sides of the cake tin and line with a double thickness of baking parchment, extending above the rim by 3cm (see page 12).

2 Peel and grate the carrots; you need 200g grated weight. Roughly chop the 120g walnuts and set aside.

3 Sift the flour, bicarbonate of soda, salt, mixed spice and cinnamon together into a large bowl.

4 Break the eggs into a medium bowl and beat lightly with a fork until broken up. Add both sugars, the oil, grated carrot, chopped walnuts, pineapple and eggs to the dry ingredients and stir to combine. Using an electric whisk, beat the mixture on a low speed for 1 minute until thoroughly mixed, but without breaking up all the pineapple and nuts.

5 Pour the mixture into the prepared tin and bake in the oven for 1½–2 hours until a skewer inserted into the centre of the cake comes out clean, or with a few moist crumbs clinging to it.

6 Leave the cake to cool in the tin for 30 minutes, then remove from the tin and leave to cool completely on a wire rack before removing the baking parchment.

7 To make the icing, finely grate the lemon zest. Sift the icing sugar into a large bowl, then add the cream cheese, butter and lemon zest. Using an electric whisk, beat until light and fluffy.

8 Using a palette knife, spread the icing over the top of the cooled cake, then decorate with the reserved walnuts.

For individual carrot cakes...

✳ Divide the mixture between two 12-hole muffin trays lined with paper muffin cases. Bake at 160°C/gas mark 3 for about 30 minutes. Makes 24.

STICKY PEACH TEA LOAF

SERVES 8–10

Oil, to grease
200g dried peaches
75ml peach juice or nectar
 (use freshly squeezed
 orange juice if you can't
 find peach)
2 tbsp water
85g skinned hazelnuts
2 eggs
110g plain flour
110g wholemeal spelt flour
Pinch of salt
1½ tsp baking powder
1 tsp ground cinnamon

1 tsp ground ginger
Pinch of freshly grated
 nutmeg
110g unsalted butter,
 softened
110g soft light brown sugar
4 tbsp buttermilk or natural
 yoghurt
1–2 tbsp water or milk

FOR THE GLAZE
4 tbsp peach jam
Finely grated zest and juice
 of ½ lemon

The tea loaf can be eaten at room temperature on the day of baking, or stored for several days, well wrapped in greaseproof paper and foil in an airtight tin, without the peach glaze. Glaze the tea loaf on the day, allowing a little time for the jam to set before serving. It is a dense, fruity loaf that is delicious by itself, or buttered and served with peach or apricot compote. You will need a 900g–1kg loaf tin.

1 Heat the oven to 180°C/gas mark 4. Oil the loaf tin, then line the base and short sides with a piece of greaseproof paper that extends over the sides (see page 11).

2 Chop the dried peaches into small pieces and put in a small pan with the peach juice and water. Bring to the boil over a medium heat, then reduce the heat and simmer gently for 2–3 minutes until tender and all of the liquid has been absorbed. Set aside to cool.

3 Spread the hazelnuts out on a baking sheet and toast in the oven for 10–15 minutes until lightly browned. Tip onto a plate and leave to cool, then roughly chop. Break the eggs into a small bowl and, using a fork, beat lightly to break them up.

4 Sift both flours, the salt, baking powder and spices together into a large bowl. Add the butter, sugar, beaten eggs and buttermilk and, using an electric whisk, beat together for about 1 minute, or until well blended. Stir the soaked peaches and chopped hazelnuts into the mixture, which should be a soft dropping consistency (see page 16). If it is too stiff, add the water or milk to loosen it slightly.

5 Pile the mixture into the prepared loaf tin and level the top with the back of the spoon. Bake in the middle of the oven for 1–1¼ hours, or until well risen and golden, and a skewer inserted into the centre comes out clean, or with only a few moist crumbs clinging to it.

6 Remove from the oven and allow the cake to cool in the tin for 5–10 minutes before turning it out onto a wire rack. Remove the greaseproof paper and leave to cool.

7 To make the glaze, heat the peach jam, lemon zest and juice in a small pan over a low heat until just bubbling, then sieve into a bowl. Brush the top and sides of the tea loaf generously with the peach glaze and allow to set for 15–20 minutes before serving.

BEETROOT CAKE

MAKES two 450g tea loaves

Oil, to grease
250g beetroot, cooked
   and peeled
225g self-raising flour
1 tsp baking powder

½ tsp ground mixed spice
4 eggs
225ml sunflower oil
225g caster sugar
85g sultanas

Beetroot gives this cake a delicious moist crumb and works well with the spices. The flavour is quite subtle, so don't be put off! It's a really lovely winter cake. You will need two 450–500g loaf tins.

1 Heat the oven to 180°C/gas mark 4. Oil the 2 loaf tins, then line the base and short sides with a piece of greaseproof paper that extends over the sides (see page 11).

2 Grate the beetroot using a fine grater.

3 Sift the flour, baking powder and mixed spice into a large bowl, then stir in the grated beetroot.

4 Break the eggs into a medium bowl and beat lightly using a fork, then add the oil and sugar. Add this mixture to the flour and beetroot with the sultanas, and mix together until well combined.

5 Divide the mixture between the prepared loaf tins and bake in the middle of the oven for 50–60 minutes until a skewer inserted into the centre comes out clean.

6 Remove from the oven and leave the cakes to cool in the tins for 15–20 minutes, then turn out onto a wire rack, peel away the lining paper and leave to cool completely.

CHOCOLATE BIRTHDAY CAKE

SERVES 16–20

Oil or butter, to grease
285g plain flour
3 tbsp good quality
    cocoa powder
1½ tsp bicarbonate of soda
1½ tsp baking powder
225g caster sugar
3 eggs, at room temperature
225ml corn or sunflower oil
225ml milk
3 tbsp golden syrup

FOR THE ICING
85g butter
6 tbsp good quality
    cocoa powder
225g icing sugar
4–6 tbsp milk

TO DECORATE (OPTIONAL)
2 tubes of Smarties
1 packet of multi-coloured
    fondant icing

This fail-safe chocolate cake is great for a children's or adult's birthday party. It is made in a square tin to make it easier to cut into portions. The cake keeps well, and even improves if made a day ahead. Just keep it in an airtight container until you are ready to ice it. Feel free to change the Smartie decoration. You will need a 20–23cm square cake tin, 5cm deep.

1 Heat the oven to 170°C/gas mark 3. Lightly grease the cake tin, line with greaseproof paper and grease again (see page 11).

2 Sift the flour, cocoa powder, bicarbonate of soda, baking powder and caster sugar into a large mixing bowl.

3 Break the eggs into a separate bowl and beat using a fork, to break them up. Add the oil, milk and golden syrup and stir with a whisk until well combined.

4 Make a well in the centre of the dry ingredients, then slowly add the wet ingredients, gradually incorporating them with the whisk until you have a smooth batter. It will be runnier than a normal cake mixture.

5 Pour the mixture into the prepared tin and bake in the middle of the oven for about 40 minutes until a skewer inserted into the centre of the cake comes out clean, or with only a few moist crumbs sticking to it.

6 Remove from the oven and leave the cake to cool in the tin for 10 minutes, before transferring to a wire rack to cool. Remove the lining paper once cooled. If the cake has peaked a little in the centre, carefully trim the domed part off the cooled cake before icing it.

7 To make the icing, melt the butter in a saucepan, then remove from the heat and stir in the cocoa powder. Sift the icing sugar into a bowl, then add it to the pan along with 4 tbsp of the milk. Stir well using a small whisk until smooth, with a thick, floodable consistency. Add the remaining milk only if it is too thick.

8 Cut the cooled cake in half horizontally, using a serrated bread knife (see page 19). Spread one third of the icing over the bottom half of the cake, then replace the top half. Pour the remaining icing over the top of the cake, using a palette knife to smooth it over the top and sides of the cake. Transfer to a serving plate or a cake board.

9 Decorate the sides of the cake with Smarties, then roll out the coloured fondant and cut out letters or shapes to decorate the top of the cake as desired. Cut into squares to serve.

4
TEA LOAVES AND TRAYBAKES

These traybakes and tea loaves draw on all the different cake-making methods, but the one thing they all have in common is that they are relatively quick and simple to make, and are ideal recipes for novice bakers.

Stored in an airtight container, they will keep well for several days, many even improving over time. They are also easy to cut into portions, making them ideal for picnics and lunch boxes.

In many of these recipes, the butter and sugar are melted together rather than being beaten and aerated, which results in a moist, fudgy texture that makes many of these bakes suitable to serve warm as a pudding. Since they rise using artificial raising agents, they often include darker, stronger flavoured sugars, which mask the flavour of these agents.

CHOCOLATE AND ORANGE MARBLED LOAF CAKE

SERVES 6–8

Oil, to grease
2 small oranges
170g butter, softened
170g caster sugar
3 eggs, at room temperature

170g self-raising flour
1–2 tbsp water or milk
1 tbsp good quality
  cocoa powder
A few drops of vanilla extract

This is a classic flavour combination that looks impressive served in slices. Alternatively, try baking the mixture in the tiny individual loaf tins you can find in cooking shops, reducing the cooking time to about 15–20 minutes, depending on the exact size of the tins. You will need a 450–500g loaf tin.

1 Heat the oven to 180°C/gas mark 4. Lightly oil the tin and line the base and short sides with a strip of greaseproof paper (see page 11). Lightly oil the paper.

2 Finely grate the zest of both oranges and set aside.

3 In a medium bowl, cream the butter and sugar together using an electric whisk or wooden spoon until pale, light and fluffy.

4 Break the eggs into a small bowl and beat lightly, using a fork, until broken up. Gradually add the egg to the creamed mixture, in several additions, beating well after each addition.

5 Sift over the flour and fold it in, using a metal spoon or a spatula. If necessary, fold in enough water or milk to give a dropping consistency (see page 16).

6 Divide the mixture between 2 bowls and sift the cocoa powder into the first, mixing it through evenly. Stir the vanilla and orange zest into the second mixture.

7 Spoon some of each flavoured mixture into the bottom of the tin, layering them alternately. Once all the mixture is in the tin, use the handle of a teaspoon to make 2 or 3 swirls through the mixture, to create the marbling effect.

8 Bake in the oven for 50–60 minutes until a skewer inserted into the centre comes out clean.

9 Remove from the oven and leave the cake to cool in the tin for 10 minutes before removing to a wire rack. Remove the lining paper and leave to cool completely.

CHOCOLATE BANANA BREAD

SERVES 8–10

85g butter, plus extra,
   softened, to grease
225g plain flour
3 tsp baking powder
½ tsp bicarbonate of soda

2 eggs
2–3 very ripe bananas,
   225g peeled weight
115g caster sugar
75g dark chocolate drops

This is the ideal way to use bananas that have become too soft to eat. Over-ripe bananas have a stonger flavour than yellow ones so are not overpowered by the chocolate in this recipe. They also make this cake deliciously moist. You will need a 900g–1kg loaf tin.

1 Heat the oven to 190°C/gas mark 5. Lightly grease the tin and line the base and short sides with a strip of greaseproof paper, then grease the paper (see page 11).

2 Melt the butter in a small pan over a gentle heat, then remove from the heat and set aside to cool until tepid.

3 Sift the flour, baking powder and bicarbonate of soda into a medium bowl.

4 Lightly beat the eggs in a bowl. Mash the bananas in another, large bowl, using a fork, then stir in the sugar, eggs and cooled melted butter.

5 Sift the dry ingredients again over the top and fold in, using a large metal spoon or a spatula. Stir in the chocolate drops.

6 Transfer the mixture to the prepared tin, smooth the top and bake for 45–50 minutes, or until a skewer inserted into the centre comes out clean.

7 Remove from the oven and leave the cake to cool in the tin for 10 minutes before removing to a wire rack. Peel off the lining paper and leave to cool completely.

HONEY LOAF CAKE

Oil, to grease
140g butter
110g soft light brown sugar
170g runny honey

2 eggs
225g self-raising flour
15g flaked almonds

This simple and delicious cake has a subtle honey flavour. You will need a 900g–1kg loaf tin.

1 Heat the oven to 180°C/gas mark 4. Lightly oil the tin and line the base and short sides with a strip of greaseproof paper (see page 11).

2 Melt the butter, sugar and honey in a saucepan over a low heat, stirring occasionally. Remove from the heat, scrape into a large bowl using a spatula, and leave to cool until tepid.

3 Break the eggs into a small bowl and whisk using a fork to break them up. Beat the eggs into the cooled honey mixture and then sift over the flour and fold in carefully, using a large metal spoon or a spatula.

4 Pour the mixture into the prepared tin and sprinkle the flaked almonds over the surface. Bake in the middle of the oven for 45–60 minutes until the top springs back when pressed lightly with a fingertip.

5 Remove from the oven and leave the cake to cool in the tin for 10 minutes, then turn out onto a wire rack, remove the paper and leave to cool completely before slicing.

FRUIT
TEA LOAF

MAKES 2; EACH SERVES 5–6

225g pitted dried dates
290ml hot Earl Grey tea
85g plain flour
3 tsp baking powder
2 tsp ground cinnamon
85g wholemeal flour

225g dried apples, chopped
170g dried cranberries or
   dried sour cherries
170g raisins
55g ground almonds
6 tbsp apple juice

This is a dairy-free cake that contains no refined sugar. The dates need to be soaked overnight in order to plump up and give the cake its characteristic moist texture. You will need two 450–500g loaf tins.

1 Roughly chop the dates and put in a heatproof bowl. Brew the tea, pour over the dates and leave to soak overnight.

2 The following day, heat the oven to 170°C/gas mark 3. Line the base and sides of the loaf tins with a strip of baking parchment (see page 11).

3 Sift the plain flour, baking powder and cinnamon into a large bowl. Add the wholemeal flour, dried apples, dried cranberries or cherries, raisins and ground almonds and stir well.

4 Add the apple juice to the date mixture and stir into the dry ingredients. Mix until well combined.

5 Divide the mixture between the tins and bake in the middle of the oven for 45 minutes, or until a skewer inserted into the centre comes out clean.

6 Remove from the oven and leave the cakes in the tins for 10 minutes, then turn out and place on a wire rack. Leave to cool completely, peeling off the parchment when the cake is nearly cool.

MARMALADE LOAF CAKE

SERVES 8–10

Oil, to grease
1 orange
2 eggs, at room temperature
170g butter, softened
85g soft light brown sugar

6 tbsp orange marmalade
100g raisins
225g self-raising flour
150g icing sugar

The flavour of this cake will vary depending on the marmalade you use; a thick-cut, old-fashioned marmalade will give the deepest and most distinctive flavour, whereas a pale variety with no shreds will result in a much subtler, gently orangey cake. You will need a 900g–1kg loaf tin.

1 Heat the oven to 180°C/gas mark 4. Lightly oil the tin and line the base and short sides with a strip of greaseproof paper (see page 11). Finely grate the orange zest and squeeze the juice; set aside separately.

2 Break the eggs into a small bowl and beat using a fork to break them up.

3 In a large bowl, cream together the butter and sugar using an electric whisk or a wooden spoon, until pale and fluffy. Gradually add the eggs, beating well after each addition. Stir in the orange zest, 2 tbsp of the juice (reserve the rest), the marmalade and the raisins.

4 Sift over the flour and fold in, using a large metal spoon or a spatula. Transfer the mixture to the prepared tin and bake in the middle of the oven for 35–45 minutes until a skewer inserted into the centre comes out clean, or with only a few moist crumbs clinging to it.

5 Remove from the oven and leave the cake to cool in the tin for 15 minutes before turning it out onto a wire rack and peeling off the lining paper. Leave to cool completely.

6 To make the icing, sift the icing sugar into a bowl and heat the remaining reserved orange juice in a small pan. Stir enough of the hot juice into the icing sugar to make a fairly stiff coating consistency, starting with just a teaspoonful. The icing should hold a trail when dripped from a spoon.

7 Pour the icing over the cake, allowing it to drip a little down the sides, and leave to set fully before serving.

STICKY GINGERBREAD

SERVES 10	
175ml sunflower oil, plus extra to grease	1 tsp ground cinnamon
Piece of fresh root ginger	¼ tsp ground cloves
225ml Guinness or other stout beer	¼ tsp freshly grated nutmeg
225ml dark molasses	Large pinch of ground cardamom
½ tsp bicarbonate of soda	3 eggs
255g plain flour	220g dark brown sugar
1½ tsp baking powder	200g caster sugar
2 tsp ground ginger	Icing sugar, to dust

Serve this gingerbread as it is, or lightly dust with icing sugar and serve with some lightly whipped unsweetened double cream. It is much better made a day or two ahead, as this allows the flavours to develop, and it will keep for several days if closely wrapped in cling film in an airtight tin. You will need a 30 x 20cm baking tin, 5cm deep.

1 Heat the oven to 180°C/gas mark 4. Oil the baking tin and line the base and sides with baking parchment (see page 11). Peel and grate enough ginger to give 1 tbsp.

2 Bring the stout and molasses to the boil in a large saucepan. Remove from the heat and stir in the bicarbonate of soda. Set aside to cool to room temperature.

3 Sift the flour, baking powder and spices into a large bowl.

4 In a separate bowl, whisk together the eggs and the sugars, then whisk in the oil, the stout mixture and the grated ginger.

5 Add the whisked mixture to the dry ingredients and stir well until just combined.

6 Pour the batter into the prepared tin and tap sharply on the work surface to remove any large air bubbles. Bake in the middle of the oven for 50–60 minutes until a skewer inserted into the centre comes out with only a few moist crumbs sticking to it, allowing at least half the cooking time before opening the oven to check the cake.

7 Leave the gingerbread to cool in the tin for 5 minutes, then turn out onto a wire rack and allow to cool completely before removing the lining paper. Dust with icing sugar and cut into slices to serve.

ESPRESSO FUDGE BROWNIES WITH HOT MOCHA SAUCE

SERVES 8–10

170g good quality dark
  chocolate, about
  70% cocoa solids
170g unsalted butter
1¼–1½ tbsp instant espresso
  coffee granules, depending
  on taste
1 tsp vanilla extract
3 eggs
225g soft dark brown sugar
85g self-raising flour
Pinch of salt

FOR THE SAUCE
170g good quality dark
  chocolate, about
  70% cocoa solids
1 tbsp golden syrup
2 tbsp Tia Maria (or other
  coffee liqueur)
3 tbsp water
½ tbsp instant espresso
  coffee granules

Serve these brownies hot, flooded with the rich mocha sauce, and a scoop of vanilla ice cream or crème fraîche, which balances the intense chocolate and coffee flavours perfectly. You will need a 20cm square, shallow cake tin.

1 Heat the oven to 180°C/gas mark 4. Line the cake tin with baking parchment (see page 11).

2 Break the chocolate into small pieces and place in a heatproof bowl. Cut the butter into small dice and add to the chocolate with the coffee granules and vanilla. Set the bowl over a saucepan of just-boiled water, ensuring the base of the bowl is not touching the water. Give the chocolate and butter an occasional stir to encourage them to melt.

3 Break the eggs into a medium bowl, add the sugar and, using an electric whisk, beat until thick and creamy and the mixture holds a 5–6 second ribbon (see page 50).

4 Pour the warm, melted chocolate into the egg mixture and carefully fold it through using a large, metal spoon or a spatula. Don't worry if it looks a bit marbled at this stage; it is better to slightly under-mix it than to over-work it.

5 Sift the flour and salt into the bowl and fold it in quickly and lightly, trying to keep as much air as possible in the mixture.

6 Pour the mixture into the prepared tin and bake in the middle of the oven for 40–45 minutes, or until the surface is dry to the touch. Take care not to overcook the mixture or it will lose its soft, fudgy texture.

7 Leave the brownie to cool in the tin set on a wire rack for 5 minutes before lifting carefully from the tin and transferring to a wire rack to cool.

8 To make the sauce, put all the ingredients in a small heatproof bowl set over a saucepan of just-boiled water, ensuring the bowl is not touching the water. Stir occasionally while the chocolate is melting until it is smooth and shiny.

9 Cut the brownie into squares. Serve warm, or at room temperature, drizzled with the hot sauce and with a scoop of vanilla ice cream or a dollop of crème fraîche on the side.

RICH DARK CHOCOLATE BROWNIES

MAKES 20

200g good quality dark
chocolate, minimum
60% cocoa solids
140g butter

225g caster sugar
2 large eggs, plus 1 extra yolk
2 tsp vanilla extract
85g plain flour

These gorgeous brownies are for adults who enjoy an intense, dark chocolatey flavour. It is important to use a really good quality chocolate with a high percentage of cocoa solids. The brownie can also be cut into tiny squares and served as petits fours. You will need a 20cm square, shallow cake tin.

1 Heat the oven to 180°C/gas mark 4. Line the baking tin with baking parchment (see page 11).

2 Break the chocolate into small pieces and place in a large heatproof bowl. Cut the butter into small cubes and add to the chocolate. Stand the bowl over a pan of just-boiled water, making sure that the base of the bowl is not touching the water, to melt the chocolate, stirring occasionally.

3 Set aside to cool for 2–3 minutes, then whisk in the sugar using an electric whisk until well combined. Beat the eggs and yolk in a separate bowl with the vanilla extract, just to combine.

4 Gradually whisk the eggs into the chocolate mixture and beat until smoothly combined. Sift in the flour and whisk in well for about 20 seconds until the colour begins to lighten.

5 Pour the mixture into the prepared tin and bake in the middle of the oven for 25–35 minutes, or until a knife inserted in the middle comes out with moist crumbs (not wet batter) clinging to it. It is better to slightly undercook than overcook brownies, as they should still be fudgy in the middle and will become less moist as they cool.

6 Leave to cool in the tin for 2 minutes before lifting carefully from the tin and transferring to a wire rack to cool. Remove the paper before the brownie is completely cold. Cut into 20 squares using a sharp knife. These are delicious served cold or warmed through and served with ice cream as a dessert.

CHOCOLATE BROWNIES WITH CREAM CHEESE SWIRL

MAKES 16

85g good quality dark
 chocolate, ideally
 70% cocoa solids
110g unsalted butter
2 eggs, at room temperature
200g caster sugar
½ tsp vanilla extract
85g plain flour
Pinch of salt

FOR THE CREAM CHEESE SWIRL
200–225g full-fat cream
 cheese, softened
50g caster sugar
1 egg yolk
¼ tsp vanilla extract

Here, cream cheese lends a delicious sweet and salty flavour to a rich chocolate brownie. Try flavouring the cream cheese with orange zest for another classic flavour combination. You will need a 20cm square baking tin.

1 Heat the oven to 180°C/gas mark 4. Line the baking tin with baking parchment (see page 11).

2 Break the chocolate into small pieces and place in a large heatproof bowl. Cut the butter into small pieces and add to the chocolate. Stand the bowl over a saucepan of just-boiled water, ensuring the base of the bowl is not touching the water. Give the chocolate and butter an occasional stir to encourage them to melt. Once melted, remove the bowl from the pan and leave to cool slightly.

3 Break the eggs into a small bowl and lightly beat with a fork to break them up.

4 Stir the sugar, eggs and vanilla into the melted chocolate mixture until well combined. Sift the flour and salt over the mixture and stir until smooth, then pour into the prepared tin.

5 In a small bowl, whisk together the cream cheese, sugar, egg yolk and vanilla until smooth. Spoon dollops of the mixture over the brownie batter, then swirl into the batter using a knife or spatula, to marble the mixtures.

6 Bake in the oven for 25–35 minutes until a skewer inserted into the centre comes out with just a few moist crumbs on it.

7 Leave to cool in the tin set on a wire rack until almost cold. Carefully remove from the tin, peel off the lining paper and cut into squares.

PECAN FUDGE BLONDIES

MAKES 18

150g pecan nuts
140g vanilla fudge
3 eggs, at room temperature
170g unsalted butter, softened
75g caster sugar

150g soft light brown sugar
½ tsp vanilla extract
200g plain flour
1 tsp baking powder
Pinch of salt

Classic blondies have a fudge-like flavour, achieved here with the brown sugar and vanilla combination as well as the pieces of actual fudge stirred in. These have the great flavour of pecan pie without the need for pastry making! You will need a shallow 30 x 32cm baking tin.

1 Heat the oven to 180°C/gas mark 4. Line the baking tin with baking parchment (see page 11).

2 Spread the pecan nuts out on a separate baking tray and toast in the oven for 10–15 minutes. Tip onto a plate to cool, then roughly chop the nuts.

3 Cut the fudge into very small dice. Break the eggs into a small bowl and, using a fork, beat lightly to break them up. Set aside.

4 Cream the butter and sugars together in a medium bowl until pale and fluffy, using an electric whisk. Add the eggs in several additions, beating well after each addition, then stir in the vanilla, using a large metal spoon or a spatula.

5 Sift in the flour, baking powder and salt and add the chopped pecans and all but 1 tbsp of the fudge. Stir well to combine.

6 Spoon the mixture into the prepared tin and scatter the remaining fudge over the surface. Bake in the middle of the oven for about 30 minutes until a skewer inserted into the centre comes out clean, or with a few moist crumbs still clinging to it.

7 Remove from the oven and leave to cool in the tin set on a wire rack. Remove when almost cooled and peel away the lining paper. Cut into squares while still warm.

PEANUT BUTTER BLONDIES

MAKES 16

225g unsalted butter, softened
350g caster sugar
255g smooth peanut butter
2 eggs, plus 1 extra yolk, at room temperature

2 tsp vanilla extract
250g self-raising flour
Pinch of salt
225g dark chocolate buttons

Blondies share the same fudgy texture as a brownie, but sugar, and in this case peanut butter, replaces chocolate as the predominant flavour. As when making brownies, it is always better to slightly undercook them to ensure a gooey, fudge-like consistency. You will need a 24cm square, shallow baking tin.

1 Heat the oven to 180°C/gas mark 4. Line the baking tin with baking parchment (see page 11).

2 Cream together the butter and sugar until pale and fluffy, using an electric whisk, then add the peanut butter and beat again until well combined.

3 Break the eggs and extra yolk into a small bowl and beat with a fork. Add to the mixture with the vanilla and mix until well combined. Sift over the flour and salt, then mix on the lowest speed until just combined.

4 Stir in the chocolate buttons, then spoon the mixture into the prepared tin. Bake in the middle of the oven for 35–40 minutes until a deep golden colour and a skewer inserted into the centre comes out with a few moist crumbs still clinging to it.

5 Remove from the oven and leave to cool in the tin set on a wire rack, before removing and slicing into squares.

FLAPJACKS

MAKES 16

150g butter, plus extra to
    grease
100g soft light brown sugar

50g golden syrup
200g rolled oats

**This is one of our favourite standby recipes. Made
from ingredients you are likely to have to hand, these
flapjacks can be mixed, baked and ready to eat in
next to no time. You will need a 20cm square, shallow
baking tin.**

1 Heat the oven to 190°C/gas mark 5. Lightly grease the
baking tin.

2 Put the butter into a saucepan and melt over a gentle heat.
Add the sugar and syrup and stir for 2 minutes to warm
through rather than melt.

3 Remove the pan from the heat and add the oats. Stir
thoroughly, then spread the mixture evenly in the tin.

4 Bake in the oven for 20–25 minutes, or until golden brown.

5 Remove from the oven and, using a sharp knife, cut the
flapjack into 16 squares while still warm. Leave in the tin to
cool for 10 minutes before transferring to a wire rack to cool
completely. These bars will keep for 4–5 days, stored in an
airtight container.

MALTED DATE AND OAT SQUARES

MAKES 16

170g butter
100g soft light brown sugar
60g malt extract
60g ready-to-eat stoned
    dates

200g rolled oats
4 tbsp Horlicks or similar
    malted drink powder

Malt extract is sweet and syrupy, and can be bought from most health food shops. Try adding 1 tbsp of your favourite seeds or chopped nuts along with the oats. Walnuts, sunflower and sesame seeds would all work well. You will need a 20cm square, shallow baking tin.

1 Heat the oven to 180°C/gas mark 4. Line the baking tin with baking parchment (see page 11).

2 Melt the butter, sugar and malt extract in a saucepan over a gentle heat, stirring until the butter has melted and the mixture is hot, then remove from the heat.

3 Roughly chop the dates and add them to the pan along with the oats and Horlicks, and stir thoroughly.

4 Spread the date and oat mixture evenly in the tin and bake for 20–25 minutes until evenly browned.

5 Remove from the oven and use a sharp knife to score the traybake into 16 squares while still warm. Leave to cool in the tin for 5 minutes before removing from the tin and taking off the parchment. Cut through the squares while still a little warm, then transfer to a wire rack and leave to cool completely.

CHRISTMAS FRIDGE CAKE

SERVES 10–12

50g dried cherries or
   cranberries, or a mixture
50ml Grand Marnier,
   Cointreau or Port (or
   orange juice if you prefer
   not to use alcohol)
125g butter
2 tbsp golden syrup
2 tbsp good quality
   cocoa powder
1 tsp ground cinnamon
220g digestive biscuits

80g pecan nuts or almonds
125g Christmas cake or
   Christmas pudding

**FOR THE CHOCOLATE
TOPPING**
75g butter
250g dark chocolate,
   minimum 60%
   cocoa solids
3 tbsp double cream

This cake is ideal for those who like the flavours of Christmas baking, but find the traditional cake too rich. It's also a great way to use up the last slice of cake after Christmas! It is best to start this cake a day in advance, to allow the dried fruit to soak up all the flavour of the liqueur. Try cutting into tiny squares to serve as a petit four with coffee over the festive season. You will need a 30 x 20cm shallow baking dish or tin.

1 Put the dried cherries or cranberries into a small bowl and pour over the liqueur or orange juice. Leave to soak for at least 2 hours, ideally overnight.

2 Line the baking dish or tin with baking parchment (see page 11).

3 Melt the butter in a small saucepan with the syrup, cocoa powder and cinnamon. Stir to combine, remove from the heat and set aside.

4 Put the biscuits and nuts in a medium bowl and crush, using the end of a rolling pin or your hands. Larger lumps are fine, as they will give the cake a crunchy texture. Crumble in the Christmas cake or pudding.

5 Pour the dried fruit and soaking liquor into the melted chocolate mixture, stir well, then pour into the biscuit mixture. Stir until well combined, then scrape into the prepared dish and smooth out evenly using the back of a wooden spoon. Cover the surface with cling film and refrigerate.

6 Meanwhile, to make the topping, slowly heat the butter, chocolate and cream in a small saucepan, stirring occasionally until completely melted, then remove from the heat and leave to cool to room temperature.

7 Pour the topping over the chilled base and tilt the dish from side to side, to encourage the topping to spread evenly. Refrigerate again for at least 2 hours before carefully transferring to a chopping board and slicing into squares.

RASPBERRY AND LIME TRAYBAKE

MAKES 12 squares

FOR THE LIME DOUGH
1 lime
175g unsalted butter, softened
75g caster sugar
Few drops of vanilla extract
250g plain flour

FOR THE CRUMBLE TOPPING
75g unsalted butter
110g plain flour
Pinch of salt
75g caster sugar

FOR THE RASPBERRY FILLING
2 punnets of raspberries (250–300g)
15–20g caster sugar, to taste

The use of fresh raspberries rather than jam gives this slice an intense fruity flavour, which is enhanced by a hint of lime. Use frozen raspberries if fresh are unavailable or expensive. You will need a 23cm square, or 30 x 20cm, deep, lipped baking tray.

1 Line the baking tray with baking parchment (see page 11). Finely grate the lime zest and squeeze the juice; set both aside.

2 Cream the butter and sugar together in a medium bowl, using an electric whisk, until light and fluffy. Add the vanilla and the lime zest, then gradually stir in the flour and mix to a smooth dough, using a wooden spoon.

3 Transfer the mixture to the prepared tray and press into an even layer, making sure the dough is pushed well into the corners; you may need to flour your hands a little to do this.

4 Chill in the fridge for 20–30 minutes until firm to the touch. Heat the oven to 180°C/gas mark 4.

5 To make the filling, put the raspberries in a bowl and sprinkle over the sugar and a little lime juice. Allow the flavours to mingle for at least 15 minutes then, using the back of a large spoon, break the raspberries up to create a compote; it does not need to be smooth. Taste and adjust the sugar and lime if necessary.

6 Bake the shortbread in the oven for 25–30 minutes until cooked through and a pale golden colour. Remove from the oven and set aside to cool in the tray. Increase the oven temperature to 200°C/gas mark 6.

7 To make the crumble topping, cut the butter into small cubes and put into a small bowl. Sift in the flour and salt. Rub the butter into the flour using your fingertips until it resembles coarse breadcrumbs. Don't worry if it starts to clump together a little. Add the sugar and mix well.

8 Transfer the raspberry mixture to a sieve set over a bowl, to drain off as much of the juice as possible. Spread the compote onto the shortbread in an even layer, then sprinkle the topping over the compote in a thin, even layer.

9 Bake in the oven for 20–25 minutes until the crumble is golden brown, then remove to a wire rack to cool in the tray. Once cool, carefully lift it out onto a board and cut into squares or rectangles.

PEAR AND WALNUT CRUMBLE CAKE

MAKES 12 slices

Oil, to grease
4 firm pears
3 tbsp Calvados
170g butter, softened
170g caster sugar
3 eggs, at room temperature
170g self-raising flour
1 tsp ground cinnamon
1 tsp ground mixed spice
2 tbsp demerara sugar
Icing sugar, to dust

FOR THE CRUMBLE TOPPING
30g butter
55g plain flour
55g caster sugar
1 tsp ground cinnamon
75g walnuts

The sweet cinnamon crumble topping complements pear and apple alike, so do try the variation too. This recipe also works very well if apples and pecans are used in place of the classic pear and walnut combination. You will need a 25 x 22cm roasting tin (or other tin with similar dimensions).

1 Heat the oven to 190°C/gas mark 5. Line the roasting tin with greaseproof paper and brush lightly with oil. Peel and core the pears, coarsely grate one of them and mix with 2 tbsp of the Calvados. Cut the remaining 3 pears into 1–2cm slices and set aside.

2 To make the crumble topping, rub the butter into the flour in a medium bowl, then stir in the sugar and cinnamon. Roughly chop the walnuts and stir them in.

3 To make the cake, cream the butter and caster sugar together in a medium bowl, using an electric whisk or wooden spoon, until pale and fluffy.

4 Break the eggs into a small bowl and beat using a fork to break them up. Gradually add the eggs to the creamed mixture, beating well between each addition.

5 Sift over the flour and spices, stir in the grated pear with its Calvados, and pour the mixture into the prepared tin. Smooth the top with a spatula.

6 Sprinkle half the crumble topping on top of the cake mixture, arrange the sliced pears on top and drizzle over the remaining 1 tbsp Calvados. Cover with the remaining crumble mixture and sprinkle over the demerara sugar.

7 Bake for 60–70 minutes until it feels firm on top and a skewer inserted into the centre comes out with a few moist crumbs still clinging to it.

8 Leave the cake to cool in the tin for 5–10 minutes, then transfer to a wire rack to cool completely. Remove the greaseproof paper and dust with icing sugar just before serving.

Variation

✳ **Apple and pecan crumble cake** Replace the pears with apples and the walnuts with pecans.

LEMON CURD SHORTCAKE

MAKES 12 bars

110g butter, plus extra
   to grease
225g self-raising flour,
   plus extra to dust
85g caster sugar

1 egg
½ tsp vanilla extract
4 generous tbsp lemon curd
   (see page 40 or use good
   quality shop bought)

Don't worry if the surface of this shortcake looks a little haphazard before it goes in the oven. Any texture on the dough will be transformed into golden brown crispness, which looks very appetising once it is baked. You will need a 30 x 20cm shallow baking tin.

1 Heat the oven to 190°C/gas mark 5. Lightly grease the baking tin.

2 Sift the flour into a medium bowl. Cut the butter into small cubes, add to the flour and rub in gently using your fingertips, until the mixture becomes a uniform fine, pale crumb with no visible lumps of butter. Stir in the sugar.

3 Break the egg into a small bowl and beat lightly with a fork until broken up, then beat in the vanilla. Sprinkle the egg into the crumb and, using a cutlery knife, quickly distribute it throughout. Bring the mixture together to make a soft dough.

4 Divide the dough in half and press one half of the dough evenly into the prepared tin. Spread the lemon curd evenly over the top.

5 Lightly flour the work surface and your hands and press the remaining half of the dough into a rectangle roughly the same size as the tin.

6 Very gently place this rectangle of dough on the lemon curd to make a sandwich, easing the mixture out to the sides to cover the lemon curd. It doesn't matter if there is a small gap. If the dough is too soft to lift in one piece, then place strips of it on the top of the curd and smooth the strips together with your finger. Alternatively, chill the dough in the freezer until firm and grate it over the surface of the curd.

7 Bake in the oven for 5 minutes, then lower the oven setting to 150°C/gas mark 2 and continue to bake for 20–25 minutes until pale golden and cooked, with no grey patches.

8 Remove from the oven and leave to cool for 10 minutes in the tin. Cut into 12 rectangles while still warm, then remove from the tin and leave to cool completely on a wire rack.

5

SMALL CAKES, SCONES AND BISCUITS

From friands, financiers and cupcakes, through fruity scones
and muffins, to chunky cookies there are plenty of tempting
teatime treats to choose from here. These recipes draw on the
important cake methods in earlier chapters, so do refer back
to the relevant sections for more detailed information
on techniques such as creaming and whisking.

BLUEBERRY AND LEMON FRIANDS

MAKES 20

195g unsalted butter
1 lemon
7 small egg whites
75g plain flour

225g icing sugar
125g ground almonds
100g blueberries

Friends are typically baked in oval moulds or individual loaf tins and are often flavoured with fruits, chocolate or flavoured oils. You will need 20 individual oval or rectangular moulds (or you can use fewer moulds and bake the friands in smaller batches).

1 Heat the oven to 200°C/gas mark 6. Melt 20g of the butter in a small saucepan over a low heat. Place the moulds on a baking tray, brush each with the melted butter and set aside.

2 Melt the remaining butter over a low heat, then remove from the heat and allow to cool.

3 Finely grate the lemon zest and set aside. Whisk the egg whites in a medium bowl until frothy.

4 Sift the flour and icing sugar onto the egg whites, then sprinkle over the ground almonds and lemon zest.

5 Pour in the melted butter and, using a large metal spoon, fold all the ingredients together until they are well mixed with no streaks of butter or lumps of flour. Fold in the blueberries.

6 Fill the moulds about three quarters full with the mixture and bake in the oven for 15–20 minutes until risen a little and golden just around the edges. They should feel spongy when pressed lightly and your finger should not leave an indentation.

7 Remove from the oven and allow to cool for 5 minutes before releasing the cakes from the tins using the tip of a sharp knife. Turn out onto a wire rack to cool completely. These are best eaten the same day you make them.

Variations

✻ **Plain friands** Simply omit the blueberries.

✻ **Dried cherry friands** Replace the fresh blueberries with 75g dried cherries.

FINANCIERS

MAKES about 20

95g unsalted butter
50g skinned hazelnuts
  or almonds
50g plain flour
100g caster sugar
Pinch of salt

4 egg whites
½ tsp vanilla extract
Small handful of fresh
  or dried cherries, or
  blueberries (optional)

Financiers are traditionally baked in individual loaf tins to resemble gold bars, hence the name. They rely on the flavour of the butter, which is melted and taken to a light caramelisation or 'beurre noisette' imparting a deep nutty flavour to the cake. You will need 20 large (7cm) individual loaf tins or barquette moulds.

1 Heat the oven to 200°C/gas mark 6.

2 Melt 20g of the butter in a small saucepan over a low heat. Place 20 large barquette moulds on a baking tray and brush each with the melted butter.

3 Melt the remaining butter over a low to medium heat and cook to a deep beurre noisette (see page 155). Remove from the heat and set aside to cool.

4 Grind the nuts to fine crumbs in a food processor. Sift the flour, ground nuts, sugar and salt into a large bowl.

5 In a separate bowl, lightly beat the egg whites until frothy, then carefully fold them into the dry ingredients, adding the beurre noisette and vanilla extract once most of the whites have been incorporated.

6 Fill each barquette mould almost to the top with the mixture and scatter the fruit, if using, over the surface. Bake in the middle of the oven for 10–15 minutes until golden brown and spongy when pressed.

7 Remove from the oven and leave the financiers to cool for a few minutes, before releasing the tops with the tip of a sharp knife. Turn out onto a wire rack and leave to cool completely. These are best eaten the same day, but will keep in an airtight container for a few days.

MADELEINES

MAKES about 36

180g butter
3 eggs
150g demerara sugar

15g clear honey
150g plain flour
1½ tsp baking powder

Madeleines are made from a type of Genoise mixture (see page 60), traditionally baked in shell-shaped baking moulds. You will need a 15–18 hole ridged madeleine tray.

1 Melt 30g of the butter in a pan over a low heat and lightly grease the madeleine tray. (Keep the rest of the melted butter for the second batch.)

2 Melt the remaining 150g butter in a second small pan over a low to medium heat and cook it to a beurre noisette (see page 155). Remove from the heat.

3 Break the eggs into a large bowl, add the sugar and honey and whisk together, using a hand-held electric whisk, until the mixture is pale and thick. It should just leave a ribbon trail when you lift the whisk (see page 50).

4 Add the flour to the beurre noisette slowly, beating with a wooden spoon to incorporate fully. Cook, stirring, over a low heat for 1 minute, then remove from the heat and set aside to cool slightly.

5 Stir this beurre noisette and flour mixture into the whisked egg mixture along with the baking powder and place in the fridge for 1 hour to firm up. Meanwhile, heat the oven to 200°C/gas mark 6.

6 Place a teaspoonful of the mixture in each madeleine mould. Bake in the middle of the oven for 8–10 minutes until risen and pale golden with a 'peaked' middle.

7 Remove the madeleines from their moulds to a wire rack to cool and repeat with the remaining mixture to cook a second batch. These are best eaten the day they are made, but will keep in an airtight container for a few days.

For mini madeleines...

✱ Bake the madeleine mixture in petits fours moulds, allowing just 4–5 minutes in the oven.

VANILLA CUPCAKES
WITH CREAM CHEESE FROSTING

MAKES 12

3 eggs, at room temperature
175g butter, softened
175g caster sugar
1 vanilla pod
175g self-raising flour
Pinch of salt
1–2 tbsp water or milk

FOR THE FROSTING
125g unsalted butter,
  softened
150g icing sugar
300g full-fat cream cheese,
  chilled
½ tsp vanilla extract

TO DECORATE (OPTIONAL)
Raspberries or blueberries
Chocolate shavings

This recipe was devised as a wedding cake alternative with the decorated cupcakes piled high on a tiered cake stand to great effect. Serve them just as they are for teatime, or decorate with a few ripe raspberries or blueberries and, or chocolate shavings. For a tiered wedding cake, sugar paste flowers are very effective. You will need a 12-hole muffin tin.

1 Heat the oven to 180°C/gas mark 4. Line the muffin tin with paper cupcake cases.

2 Break the eggs into a small bowl and, using a fork, beat lightly to break them up. Put the butter and sugar in a medium bowl. Cut the vanilla pod in half lengthways, scrape out the seeds and add to the butter and sugar.

3 Using a wooden spoon or electric whisk, cream the butter and sugar together until pale, light and fluffy.

4 Gradually add the beaten eggs in several additions, beating well after each addition.

5 Sift the flour over the surface, add the salt and fold in using a large metal spoon or a spatula. If necessary, fold in enough of the water or milk to create a dropping consistency.

6 Divide the mixture equally between the prepared cupcake cases and bake in the middle of the oven for 12–15 minutes,

or until well risen and golden. They should be springy to the touch and a skewer inserted into the centre should come out clean. Remove the cakes from the tin and cool on a wire rack.

7 Meanwhile, to make the cream cheese frosting, put the butter in a bowl and beat briefly with an electric whisk until very smooth. Sift in the icing sugar and continue to beat until completely incorporated. Add the cream cheese and vanilla, and beat the mixture for up to 1 minute until smooth and even.

8 Top each cooled cupcake with the cream cheese frosting, using a palette knife to smooth the surface, or pipe it on in a decorative swirl, using a piping bag fitted with a large star nozzle. Serve the cupcakes plain or topped with berries and/or chocolate shavings.

A note on making cupcakes in large quantities...

✱ This recipe works well when the quantities are doubled and made in a kitchen mixer (such as a Kenwood or KitchenAid), but making more than double the mixture when using domestic mixers and ovens tends not to result in the same light cakes.

MUSCOVADO AND SALTED CARAMEL CUPCAKES

MAKES 10–12

100g unsalted butter
170g dark muscovado sugar
2 eggs, at room temperature
1 tsp vanilla extract
200g self-raising flour
Pinch of salt
1–2 tbsp water or milk
  (optional)

FOR THE SALTED CARAMEL
140g caster sugar
100ml water
75ml double cream
1 level tsp flaked sea salt
½ vanilla pod

FOR THE BUTTERCREAM
170g unsalted butter,
  softened
200g icing sugar
Squeeze of lemon juice

These richly flavoured cupcakes are delicious with a cup of coffee to cut through the sweetness. You will need a 12-hole muffin tin.

1 Heat the oven to 180°C/gas mark 4. Line the muffin tin with paper cupcake cases.

2 Cream the butter and sugar together in a medium bowl, with an electric whisk or wooden spoon, until pale and fluffy. (This takes a while, so persevere.)

3 Break the eggs into a small bowl and beat lightly using a fork, to break up. Add the egg to the creamed mixture in additions, beating well between each addition, then beat in the vanilla.

4 Sift the flour with the salt over the mixture and carefully fold in, using a large metal spoon or a spatula, trying not to beat out any air. The mixture should be a soft, dropping consistency (see page 16). If it is too thick, add a little water or milk to loosen it slightly.

5 Spoon the mixture into the cupcake cases, filling them about three quarters full. Bake in the middle of the oven for about 12–15 minutes, or until they are well risen, golden brown and spring back when pressed gently with your fingertips. Remove from the oven and transfer the cupcakes to a wire rack to cool.

6 Meanwhile, to make the salted caramel, put the sugar and water in a small saucepan and place over a low heat to dissolve

the sugar, using the handle of a wooden spoon to gently agitate the sugar and to prevent it from 'caking' on the bottom of the pan. Try to avoid splashing the syrup up the sides of the pan. Once the sugar has dissolved, increase the heat and bring the syrup to the boil, without stirring. Boil until the sugar turns a deep golden brown colour. You may need to swirl the pan very gently from time to time, but do not stir.

7 Immediately pour the cream into the caramel, taking care as it will sputter and spit. Add the sea salt and the seeds from the vanilla pod and swirl the caramel in the pan to distribute the flavourings. Pour the caramel into a jug and allow to cool to tepid while you make the buttercream.

8 Put the butter and icing sugar in a medium bowl and, using an electric whisk or a wooden spoon, beat together until pale and fluffy. Add a squeeze of lemon juice and beat again briefly.

9 Check the caramel is tepid and thickened to the consistency of golden syrup. If it is too hot, it will melt the butter and curdle the icing. If too cold, it may set in lumps in the buttercream. Pour the caramel into the buttercream and beat the mixture, using a wooden spoon, until thoroughly incorporated.

10 Put this caramel icing into a piping bag fitted with a small star nozzle and pipe onto the cupcakes. Or, spread the icing on top of the cakes, using a palette knife dipped in boiling water. Allow the icing to set for 10–15 minutes before serving.

MUSCAT SPONGES
WITH ELDERFLOWER ICING

MAKES 12

3 eggs, at room temperature
170g unsalted butter,
    softened
170g icing sugar
4 tbsp Muscat or other sweet
    dessert wine
170g self-raising flour

FOR THE ICING
200g icing sugar
2 tbsp elderflower cordial
A little boiling water

These are delicate little sponge cakes, the perfect addition to any afternoon tea celebration. You will need a 12-hole muffin tin.

1 Heat the oven to 180°C/gas mark 4. Line a 12-hole muffin tin with paper cupcake cases.

2 Separate the eggs (see page 8). Put the butter and icing sugar in a medium bowl and, using an electric whisk or a wooden spoon, cream together until pale and fluffy. Add the egg yolks one at a time, beating well between each addition, then beat in the sweet wine.

3 Sift the flour into the bowl and fold it into the mixture, using a large metal spoon or a spatula, until just combined.

4 In a separate bowl, whisk the egg whites until they reach soft peaks (see page 9). Fold the egg whites into the creamed mixture, taking care not to beat any air out of the mixture.

5 Divide the mixture between the paper cases, filling them about three quarters full.

6 Bake in the middle of the oven for 15–20 minutes, or until the cakes are well risen, golden brown and spongy when pressed. Remove from the oven and transfer to a wire rack to cool completely.

7 To make the icing, sift the icing sugar into a large bowl. Pour the elderflower cordial into a small bowl and stir in about ½ tbsp boiling water. Add this mixture to the icing sugar and mix to a fairly soft coating consistency, using a wooden spoon. You may need to add a little more boiling water if the mixture is too thick.

8 Drizzle the icing freely over the top of the cooled sponges. It looks attractive if a little icing runs down the sides, so don't worry about being too tidy. Allow the icing to set for about 10 minutes before serving.

LAMINGTONS

MAKES 16

85g unsalted butter,
   plus extra to grease
85ml milk
3 large eggs, at room
   temperature
175g caster sugar
1 tsp vanilla extract
175g self-raising flour
Pinch of salt

FOR THE ICING
60g unsalted butter
85ml water
200g icing sugar
3 tbsp good quality
   cocoa powder
Pinch of salt

TO DECORATE
115g desiccated coconut

Lamingtons are Australia's national cake. A light and fluffy sponge coated in chocolate and coconut is a perfect combination, worthy of international fame. You will need a 20cm square cake tin.

1 Heat the oven to 180°C/gas mark 4. Grease the cake tin and line with baking parchment (see page 11).

2 Put the butter and milk in a small saucepan and heat gently until the butter has melted. Remove from the heat and leave to cool to tepid.

3 Meanwhile, break the eggs into a large mixing bowl and add the sugar. Using an electric whisk, beat the mixture for about 4 minutes until pale, frothy and doubled in volume. Slowly pour in the melted butter and milk, whisking continuously until thoroughly mixed, then add the vanilla.

4 Sift the flour and salt into the egg mixture and use the electric whisk on its lowest setting to gently mix in the flour. It is vital that you do not over-mix at this stage as this will cause the cake to become tough; the mixture will be runnier than for a regular cake.

5 Pour the mixture into the prepared tin and bake in the oven for about 25 minutes until golden brown on top and lightly springy all over when pressed. Do not open the oven door for at least 20 minutes, or you could cause the cake to sink.

6 Remove the cake from the oven and leave to cool in the tin for 10 minutes before turning out onto a wire rack. Gently peel away the baking parchment and leave to cool completely.

7 When cool, transfer the cake to a board. Trim the edges, then cut into 16 even squares.

8 To make the icing, melt the butter with the water in a small saucepan, remove from the heat and set aside.

9 In a large bowl, sift together the icing sugar, cocoa powder and salt. Stirring all the time, slowly add enough of the melted butter mixture to make a smooth, runny icing that will lightly and evenly coat the back of a wooden spoon. It needs to be thin enough to soak into the sponge, so not as thick as a regular icing.

10 Spread the coconut out on a plate. Dip the sponge squares into the chocolate icing, covering them on all sides and allowing the excess to drip off, then roll them in coconut until coated. This is a messy job, so you may find it helpful to use a fork to hold the piece of sponge while you spoon over the icing, and then use 2 forks while coating in the coconut. As each one is finished, transfer to a wire rack to dry out a little and allow the icing to set. Serve the cakes piled high on a plate for the ultimate Australian afternoon tea!

PASSION FRUIT YOGHURT CAKES

MAKES 16	
2 lemons	**PASSION FRUIT CURD**
250ml sunflower oil	4 passion fruit
250g caster sugar	1 egg
2 eggs	85g granulated sugar
250g passion fruit yoghurt	30g unsalted butter
280g self-raising flour	2 tbsp lemon juice

Flavoured with passion fruit yoghurt and topped with a tangy passion fruit curd, these little cakes are light and delicious. You will need a 16-hole muffin tin.

1 First make the passion fruit curd. Cut open each passion fruit and scoop the pulp into a sieve set over a bowl. Gently press the pulp through the sieve, discarding the pips.

2 Lightly beat the egg in a small bowl to break it up.

3 Put the beaten egg, sugar, butter, lemon juice and passion fruit juice into a small saucepan and heat gently over a low to medium heat, stirring constantly, until the mixture has thickened. Strain through a sieve and leave to cool.

4 Heat the oven to 170°C/gas mark 3. Line the muffin tin with paper muffin cases.

5 Finely grate the zest of both lemons and squeeze the juice; set aside.

6 Using an electric whisk, whisk the oil and sugar together in a large bowl until evenly blended. Whisk in the eggs until creamy, then stir in the yoghurt, lemon juice and zest.

7 Stir in the flour until it is just mixed through; do not over-stir the mixture.

8 Half fill the muffin cases with the mixture and bake in the middle of the oven for 20–35 minutes, or until a skewer inserted into the centre of a cake comes out clean.

9 Remove from the oven and allow the little cakes to cool completely before removing from the muffin cases and turning upside down on a plate. Spoon a little passion fruit curd over the cakes and serve.

Variation

✳ For a large passion fruit cake, this mixture can be baked in a prepared 22cm moule à manqué tin or round cake tin, with the cooking time increased to 35–40 minutes.

BLACKCURRANT AND POLENTA MUFFINS

MAKES 10

110g butter
100g golden caster sugar
2 eggs
50g fine polenta
2 oranges
200g plain flour

2 tsp baking powder
½ tsp bicarbonate of soda
½ tsp vanilla extract
110ml buttermilk
220g blackcurrants,
   fresh or frozen

This is a great basic recipe to use with a wide variety of fruit. Add fresh or frozen mixed berries or blueberries in place of the blackcurrants or even chopped bananas or other chopped larger soft fruit. Sprinkle with demerara sugar just before baking if you like a sweet crust. You will need a 12-hole muffin tin.

1 Heat the oven to 190°C/gas mark 5. Line the muffin tin with paper muffin cases.

2 Melt the butter and sugar in a small pan over a gentle heat, then set aside to cool. Break the eggs into a large bowl and beat lightly using a fork to break them up.

3 Put the polenta into a small bowl. Finely grate the zest of both oranges and squeeze the juice of one. Add the zest and juice to the polenta and stir well.

4 Sift the flour, baking powder and bicarbonate of soda into another large bowl.

5 Add the cooled butter and sugar to the beaten eggs, then add the vanilla and buttermilk.

6 Using a spatula, fold the cooled butter mixture and soaked polenta into the flour, then fold in the blackcurrants. Fill the muffin cases two thirds full with the mixture.

7 Bake on the middle shelf of the oven for 20 minutes, or until well risen and pale golden brown, and a skewer inserted in the centre comes out clean, or with a few moist crumbs attached. Eat warm from the oven or cool on a wire rack.

LEMON AND POPPYSEED MUFFINS

MAKES 12

120g butter	2 eggs
250g plain flour	120g soft light brown sugar
2 tsp baking powder	75ml milk
½ tsp bicarbonate of soda	3 lemons
Pinch of salt	150g icing sugar
2 tbsp poppy seeds	

Drizzled with a tangy lemon icing, these muffins are perfect to enjoy with a cup of tea. Or try one of the delicious variations. You will need a 12-hole muffin tin.

1 Heat the oven to 190°C/gas mark 5 and line the muffin tin with paper muffin cases.

2 Melt the butter in a small saucepan over a gentle heat, then set aside to cool.

3 Sift the flour, baking powder, bicarbonate of soda and salt into a large bowl. Stir in the poppy seeds and set aside. Break the eggs into a small bowl and beat lightly to break them up.

4 In another large bowl, mix together the cooled butter, sugar, beaten eggs and milk. Finely grate the zest and squeeze the juice from the lemons. Add all the zest and the juice of 2 lemons to the liquid ingredients, reserving the remaining juice.

5 Using a large metal spoon, fold the flour mixture into the lemon mixture, using as few folds as possible. The more the mixture is worked the heavier the muffins, so it needs a light touch. Fill the muffin cases two thirds full with the mixture.

6 Bake on the middle shelf of the oven for 20 minutes, or until the muffins are well risen and pale golden brown, and a wooden skewer inserted into the centre comes out clean or with a few moist crumbs attached.

7 Transfer the muffins in their paper cases to a wire rack and leave to cool.

8 Mix half the remaining lemon juice with the icing sugar to make a glacé icing. Drizzle over the cooled muffins.

Variations

✻ **Lemon blueberry muffins** Omit the poppy seeds, use the zest and juice of just 1 lemon and fold in 100g fresh blueberries just after the flour. Omit the icing.

✻ **Lemon raspberry cheesecake muffins** Omit the poppy seeds. Rather than add the lemon zest to the liquid ingredients, mix it with 150g cream cheese and 50g icing sugar. Fold 100g fresh raspberries into the mixture just after the flour. Half fill the muffin cases with the mixture, place a generous teaspoonful of lemon cream cheese in the middle of the mixture and top with the remaining muffin mixture. Omit the icing.

✻ **Apple cinnamon crumble muffins** Omit the lemons and poppy seeds. Soak 50g dried apples in 100ml apple juice for 3–4 hours, then drain, finely chop and add to the dry ingredients. Continue as for the main recipe, two thirds filling the muffin cases. Sift 100g plain flour with a good pinch of ground cinnamon, rub in 75g cold butter, then stir in 50g demerara sugar. Sprinkle this crumble mixture over the top of the muffins before they go in the oven. Omit the icing.

UPSIDE DOWN PLUM MUFFINS

MAKES 12

TO LINE THE TINS
70g unsalted butter
12 heaped tsp soft light
    brown sugar

FOR THE MUFFINS
6 small plums
300g plain flour

1 tbsp baking powder
½ tsp bicarbonate of soda
½ tsp salt
125g butter
2 eggs
175g soft light brown sugar
250g natural yoghurt
1 tsp vanilla extract

....

These muffins make a lovely breakfast, still warm from the oven. The trick is to weigh out the dry ingredients the night before, so there is even less to do the next day. When buying your fruit, choose plums that will fit comfortably into the muffin tin. Alternatively, you could use slices of soft fruit, such as peaches or nectarines. You will need a 12-hole muffin tin.

1 Heat the oven to 170°C/gas mark 3.

2 To prepare the tins, melt the butter in a small saucepan and carefully pour about 1 tbsp melted butter into each hole of the muffin tin, then add 1 heaped tsp soft brown sugar to each.

3 Halve and stone the plums, then place a halved plum cut side down in each tin.

4 Sift the flour, baking powder, bicarbonate of soda and salt into a large bowl.

5 Melt the butter in a small saucepan over a low heat, then allow to cool a little.

6 In a separate large bowl, beat together the eggs, sugar, melted butter, yoghurt and vanilla until very well combined.

7 Add these wet ingredients to the dry ingredients and, using a large metal spoon, stir to mix until there are no lumps, taking care not to over-mix or the muffins will be tough. The mixture will be thicker than a regular cake mix, and too thick to drop from a spoon.

8 Spoon the mixture into the tins on top of the fruit, dividing it equally and filling the tins. There is no need to spread the mixture out tidily as it will spread as it cooks. Bake on the middle shelf of the oven for 15–20 minutes until the tops are risen and golden brown.

9 Remove from the oven and leave to cool for 5 minutes in the tin, then turn the cakes out onto a wire rack; they should drop out easily. Serve plum side up, warm or at room temperature, preferably on the same day.

THIRTY-DAY BRAN MUFFINS

MAKES 20	
80g wheatbran	120g raisins
365g strong white bread flour	2 eggs
1 tsp salt	75ml sunflower oil
2½ tsp bicarbonate of soda	1 tsp vanilla extract
300g brown sugar	460ml milk

This is a recipe for a delicious bran muffin mixture which can be kept in the fridge for up to 30 days – so you can make a batch and have fresh raisin bran muffins for breakfast whenever you like. The mixture will need to chill overnight before you make the first batch. You will need a 12-hole muffin tin.

1 Put the bran in a large mixing bowl, then sift over the flour, salt and bicarbonate of soda.

2 Stir the sugar and raisins into the dry ingredients, stirring the raisins around well so that they are coated in flour (this helps to prevent them from sinking).

3 Break the eggs into a small bowl and beat lightly using a fork, until broken up. Beat in the oil and vanilla extract.

4 Make a well in the centre of the dry ingredients, then pour in the egg mixture followed by the milk. Stir the liquid in the centre only, gradually drawing in the dry ingredients from around the edge. Don't force the flour in; it will be incorporated automatically as you stir the liquid. Continue until all the dry ingredients have been incorporated and the mixture is smooth.

5 Transfer the mixture to a plastic container, seal with a lid and refrigerate overnight.

6 Heat the oven to 200°C/gas mark 6 and place the required number of paper muffin cases in a muffin tin.

7 Half fill the muffin cases with the mixture and bake on the middle shelf of the oven for 20–25 minutes until risen, golden brown and firm to the touch. Serve the muffins warm with butter or jam, or just as they are.

Variations

✱ Try adding ground spices and using other dried fruit in place of the raisins. Ground ginger and chopped dried pear are a lovely combination, and cranberries work well with cinnamon.

CHOCOLATE AND HAZELNUT MUFFINS

MAKES 12

12 hazelnuts
75g butter
100g soft dark brown sugar
3 tbsp golden syrup
3 eggs
2 tbsp soured cream

225g self-raising flour
45g good quality cocoa
  powder
2 tsp baking powder
12 tsp Nutella

These rich, nutty muffins taste delicious and have a wonderful soft centre. Be careful not to over-whisk the mixture, as it can make them tough. You will need a 12-hole muffin tin.

1 Heat the oven to 180°C/gas mark 4 and line the muffin tin with paper muffin cases.

2 Spread the hazelnuts out on a baking sheet and toast in the oven for 10 minutes, or until lightly browned. Tip onto a plate and set aside.

3 Melt the butter, sugar and syrup in a small pan over a low heat, stirring occasionally. Remove from the heat and set aside to cool until tepid.

4 Break the eggs into a small bowl and beat using a fork, to break them up. Beat the eggs into the cooled butter mixture together with the soured cream.

5 Sift the flour, cocoa powder and baking powder together into a large bowl. Make a well in the centre, add the wet ingredients and quickly stir into the flour, using no more than 12 strokes.

6 Half fill each muffin case with the mixture, then add 1 tsp Nutella and a toasted hazelnut to the middle of each. Top with the remaining muffin mixture.

7 Bake on the middle shelf of the oven for 15–20 minutes. Eat warm from the oven or cool on a wire rack.

WHITE CHOCOLATE AND STRAWBERRY MUFFINS

MAKES 12

85g strawberries
110g butter
140g soft light brown sugar
150ml milk
2 eggs

½ tsp vanilla extract
225g self-raising flour
½ tsp bicarbonate of soda
85g white chocolate drops

Soft light brown sugar gives these muffins a slightly caramel colour and flavour, but feel free to use caster sugar if you would rather have a paler muffin crumb. You will need a 12-hole muffin tin.

1 Heat the oven to 180°C/gas mark 4 and line the tin with paper muffin cases.

2 Chop the strawberries into roughly 1cm pieces and set aside.

3 Melt the butter and sugar in a small pan over a low heat, stirring occasionally. Remove from the heat, add the milk and leave to cool until tepid.

4 Break the eggs into a small bowl, beat using a fork and add with the vanilla to the cooled mixture.

5 Sift the flour and bicarbonate of soda into a large bowl and make a well in the centre. Add the wet mixture to the bowl and stir quickly. When almost completely stirred through, add the chopped strawberries and chocolate drops and stir again briefly until just distributed; the mixture should be quite wet.

6 Divide the mixture between the muffin cases and bake on the middle shelf of the oven for 20–25 minutes, or until a skewer inserted into the centre of one comes out clean, or with just a few crumbs of mixture clinging to it.

7 Remove from the oven and transfer the muffins to a wire rack to cool.

Variation

✳ White chocolate and raspberry muffins Replace the chopped strawberries with whole raspberries (fresh or frozen and defrosted).

SCONES

MAKES 6–8 scones

225g self-raising flour,
   plus extra to dust
½ tsp salt
60g butter
30g caster sugar
150ml milk
1 egg (optional)

TO SERVE
Clotted cream or butter
Strawberry jam

This technique uses the process of rubbing fat into flour (as for pastry), resulting in scones with a crumbly, moist texture. Best served freshly made, with West Country favourite clotted cream and jam.

1 Heat the oven to 220°C/gas mark 7. Sift a little flour over a baking sheet.

2 Sift the flour into a large bowl with the salt. Cut the butter into 1cm cubes and rub it into the flour with your fingertips until the mixture resembles coarse breadcrumbs. Stir in the sugar and make a well in the centre.

3 Pour in the milk and stir briskly using a cutlery knife until the dough starts to come together. Gather the dough with your hands; it should be soft and spongy (as shown). Avoid over-working or kneading, which can make the scones tough. Add a little more milk if the dough is too dry, but not too much as a very wet dough results in heavy, dense scones.

4 Place the dough on a lightly floured surface and pat or roll out to no less than a 3cm thickness. Dip a 5–6cm pastry cutter in flour and cut out the scones (as shown), getting as many as possible out of the dough. To ensure an even rise, cut firmly and avoid twisting the cutter as you release the scone. Place on the prepared baking sheet.

5 Push the cut dough back together (rather than squash it into a ball), and cut out more scones; these may not be quite as tender as the first rolled batch.

6 For a glossy crust, beat the egg in a small bowl with a fork, sieve it, then use to brush the top of the scones. Alternatively, for a soft crust, sprinkle with flour. Bake in the top third of the oven for 15–18 minutes, or until the scones are well risen and golden brown on top.

7 Transfer the scones to a wire rack to cool. Serve warm or just cooled, with clotted cream or butter and strawberry jam.

Variations

✳ **Date scones** Add 100g coarsely chopped dates to the mixture before the milk.

✳ **Cheese scones** Reduce the butter by half and omit the sugar. Add 75g strongly flavoured grated cheese, such as Cheddar, Gruyère or Parmesan, along with a pinch each of English mustard powder and cayenne pepper, before the milk.

SPICED MINCEMEAT BUTTERMILK SCONES

MAKES 8

225g self-raising flour,
    plus extra to dust
1 large orange
1½ tsp ground mixed spice
½ tsp salt
55g butter

15g caster sugar
150ml buttermilk
4 tbsp good quality
    mincemeat
2 tbsp milk
Demerara sugar, to sprinkle

These scones are richly flavoured and fruity, so they need only a slick of good unsalted butter to serve. Or, at Christmas, try serving them spread with a little brandy butter.

1 Heat the oven to 220°C/gas mark 7. Dust a baking sheet with flour.

2 Finely grate the orange zest and set aside. Sift the flour into a large bowl with the mixed spice and salt.

3 Cut the butter into cubes and, using your fingertips, rub it into the flour until it resembles coarse breadcrumbs, then stir in the sugar.

4 Pour the buttermilk into a jug or small bowl, add the mincemeat and orange zest and stir together, using a fork.

5 Make a well in the centre of the dry ingredients, pour in the wet mixture and, using a cutlery knife, stir briskly until it forms a soft, springy dough.

6 With lightly floured hands, gather the dough together and pat it out to a thickness of about 2.5cm. Using a small pastry cutter, dipped in a little flour to prevent it from sticking to the dough, stamp out rounds. Push the offcuts together to make an extra scone.

7 Place the scones on the prepared baking sheet and brush the tops liberally with milk, but taking care not to let the milk drip down the sides of the scones, as this may prevent them from rising properly. Sprinkle with demerara sugar and bake in the top third of the oven for 12–15 minutes, or until well risen, golden brown and cooked through.

8 Remove from the oven and transfer the scones to a wire rack to cool slightly before serving.

BLUEBERRY SCONES

MAKES 12

Oil, to grease
450g self-raising flour,
    plus extra to dust
1 tsp salt
120g butter
90g soft light brown sugar
150g fresh blueberries
60g dried blueberries
1 large lemon
300g natural yoghurt

FOR THE TOPPING
½ lemon
1½ tbsp natural yoghurt
30g porridge oats
1½ tbsp soft light brown
    sugar

These scones are delicious served warm from the oven. Break them into separate pieces along the indentations and serve with butter, lemon curd, or a little of each. They can also be served at room temperature, but are always best eaten on the day of baking. You will need a 30 x 20cm baking tray.

1 Heat the oven to 220°C/gas mark 7. Lightly oil the baking tray.

2 For the topping, finely grate the lemon zest and squeeze the juice, then add both to a small bowl with the yoghurt. Beat lightly with a fork to mix and set aside.

3 To make the scones, sift the flour into a large bowl with the salt. Cut the butter into 1cm cubes and rub into the flour using your fingertips, until the mixture resembles coarse breadcrumbs. Stir in the sugar and the fresh and dried blueberries.

4 Finely grate the lemon zest and squeeze the juice. Make a well in the centre of the dry ingredients and pour in the yoghurt, lemon zest and juice. Stir briskly using a cutlery knife until the dough starts to come together. Gather the dough with your hands; it should be soft and springy.

5 Roll or pat the dough out into a large rectangle, about 15 x 20cm and approximately 2.5cm thick. Cut into 12 squares and place the squares on the prepared tray so they are just touching each other.

6 Brush the top with the yoghurt and lemon topping mixture and sprinkle over the oats and soft light brown sugar. Bake in the top third of the oven for 30–40 minutes until well risen and golden brown. If the centre looks damp or doughy, bake for a further 5 minutes, or until cooked through. You may need to move it to a lower shelf after 30 minutes of cooking if it is getting a little too brown.

7 Remove from the oven and leave to cool in the tin for about 5 minutes, then transfer to a wire rack to cool slightly before breaking into pieces and serving.

Note

✻ If you can't find dried blueberries, use dried cherries or raisins instead.

SUGAR-CRUSTED SCONE ROUND WITH LEXIA RAISINS

SERVES 6–8

225g self-raising flour,
   plus extra to dust
½ tsp salt
55g butter
30g golden caster sugar
120g Lexia raisins
150ml buttermilk

FOR THE SUGAR CRUST
6 cubes of brown loaf sugar
Juice of ½ small orange

Lexia raisins – large, juicy raisins, native to Australia – elevate this recipe from an everyday scone to a special treat. If unavailable, use regular raisins and soak them in hot tea or fruit juice for about an hour, then drain and pat dry before using. Serve the scones warm with butter, or with jam and clotted cream for a treat.

1 Heat the oven to 220°C/gas mark 7. Dust a baking sheet with flour.

2 To prepare the sugar crust, crush the sugar cubes using a rolling pin and set aside.

3 Sift the flour into a medium bowl with the salt. Cut the butter into small cubes and rub it into the flour using your fingertips, until the mixture resembles coarse breadcrumbs. Add the sugar and raisins and mix them in lightly using your fingers.

4 Make a well in the centre of the flour mixture and pour in the buttermilk. Stir briskly with a cutlery knife, to bring the dough together. It should be soft but not too sticky to handle.

5 Gather the dough with your hands and shape it into a plump, round shape. Place on the baking sheet. Lightly flour a large knife and use it to cut the dough into 6–8 segments, scoring deeply, almost but not quite through to the baking sheet. Lightly plump up the dough with your hands, to restore the neat, round shape after cutting.

6 Brush all over with the orange juice, using a pastry brush. Sprinkle the crushed sugar cubes over the surface and gently press the sugar into the dough with your fingertips.

7 Bake in the top third of the oven for about 20 minutes, or until well risen, a good golden brown colour and cooked through. If the centre looks at all damp or doughy, bake for a further 5–10 minutes.

8 Remove the cooked scone from the oven and leave to cool on the baking sheet for 5 minutes, then transfer to a wire rack to cool slightly before serving.

CLASSIC SHORTBREAD

MAKES about 20

100g butter, softened
50g caster sugar, plus extra
   to sprinkle

130g plain flour
30g ground rice

To ensure the traditional crimped shape and markings are clearly defined once the 'petticoat tails' are baked, make sure your shaped shortbread is chilled until completely firm and the oven is fully preheated before baking. You will need a 15cm flan ring.

1 Place a 15cm flan ring on a baking sheet. Put the butter into a medium to large bowl and beat with a wooden spoon until soft, then add the sugar and beat well until fully incorporated.

2 Sift the flour and ground rice into the mixture and stir to a firm, smooth paste. You may need to use the back of the wooden spoon to 'mash' the ingredients together (as shown).

3 Press the mixture into the flan ring and smooth into a neat circle, using the back of a cutlery spoon, then remove the flan ring. Crimp the edges of the shortbread with your fingers to create a decorative edge (as shown).

4 Mark the shortbread into 8 wedges, scoring deeply with a large knife (as shown). Prick evenly with a fork well into the dough and chill until firm. Meanwhile, heat the oven to 170°C/gas mark 3.

5 Sprinkle the shortbread evenly with a little sugar and cook on the middle shelf of the oven for 20–25 minutes, or until a pale biscuit colour with no grey patches in the middle. Remove from the oven and run a palette knife under the shortbread to loosen it from the baking sheet.

6 Leave to cool for 5 minutes before transferring the shortbread to a wire rack to cool completely. It will keep for a few days in an airtight container.

Variations

✱ **Almond shortbread** Replace 50g of the plain flour with 50g ground almonds. For a crunchier texture, you can also stir 10g roughly chopped blanched almonds into the mixture.

✱ **Orange shortbread** Add the finely grated zest of ½ orange with the flour.

APRICOT POLENTA SHORTBREAD

MAKES 12 squares or 9 bars	
200g dried apricots	110g caster sugar
275g plain flour	2 eggs
¼ tsp salt	1 tsp vanilla extract
150g fine polenta	340g apricot jam
225g butter, softened	

This shortbread owes its light, crumbly texture to the addition of polenta. It is usually served at room temperature for tea, but is also lovely warm, with whipped cream or ice cream. The fruit and jam could be swapped for figs, raspberries or even dates. Or you could use Nutella as a filling and add chocolate chips to the dough. You will need a 30 x 20cm shallow baking tin.

1 Heat the oven to 180°C/gas mark 4. Line the baking tin with baking parchment (see page 11). Using a large knife, finely chop the dried apricots and set aside.

2 In a large bowl, sift together the flour, salt and polenta, ensuring that there are no lumps. Pour in any polenta that doesn't go through the sieve.

3 In a separate bowl, cream the butter and sugar together until pale and fluffy, using an electric whisk.

4 In a small bowl, beat the eggs lightly with a fork to loosen, then add to the sugar and butter a little at a time, beating well after each addition until thoroughly incorporated. Add the vanilla extract.

5 Add the dry ingredients and mix on a low speed or using a wooden spoon, until the mixture has just come together into large lumps, and there are no pockets of flour.

6 Press two thirds of the shortbread dough into the prepared tin, then use a floured wooden spoon to make the surface as even as possible.

7 Spread the jam evenly over the dough, then sprinkle the chopped apricots over the surface.

8 Break off small pieces from the remaining dough and distribute them randomly over the surface.

9 Bake on the middle shelf of the oven for about 30 minutes until the surface is golden brown and the dough is cooked through. Leave the shortbread to cool in the tin before cutting into squares or bars.

Note

✳ If the heat of the oven results in some singed pieces of apricot protruding from the cake, wait for the shortbread to cool a little before picking out the offending pieces.

MACAROONS

MAKES 50 paired macaroons

200g ground almonds
200g icing sugar
160g egg whites
   (about 5 medium)
Food colouring of your choice
   (see below)
75ml water
200g caster sugar

TO ASSEMBLE
Chocolate ganache
   (see page 153)
OR
Buttercream (see page 152)
OR
Good quality jam

1 Line 2 baking sheets with baking parchment. Thoroughly mix the ground almonds and icing sugar together in a food processor and sift into a large bowl, discarding any coarse pieces of almond remaining in the sieve.

2 Put the almond mixture into a bowl and, using a spatula, mix in 80g unbeaten egg white, to create a smooth paste. Add ¼–1 tsp food colouring, depending on how vibrant you want the colour to be. Set aside.

3 Bring the water and sugar to the boil in a small saucepan to make a sugar syrup. Meanwhile, in a large bowl, whisk the remaining 80g egg white to soft peaks using a hand-held electric whisk (see page 9). When the sugar syrup reaches 115°C, pour it over the whisked egg white, avoiding pouring it onto the whisk itself, then continue to whisk to stiff peaks.

4 Using a spatula, stir one third of this meringue into the almond paste, to loosen the mixture, then carefully fold in the remaining meringue. Continue to fold the mixture just until it becomes smooth, uniform, gently flowing and a little shiny. Test a small amount on the baking parchment: it should not be stiff enough to leave a peak, nor so soft that it floods excessively.

5 Fill a piping bag fitted with a 5–8mm plain nozzle with the macaroon mixture and pipe little mounds, about 2–2.5cm in diameter, onto the prepared trays. Set aside for 20–30 minutes until a skin forms on the surface. Meanwhile, heat the oven to 160°C/gas mark 2½.

6 To check the macaroons are ready to bake, lightly brush the top of one with the tip of your finger: the batter should not stick to your finger and it should feel slightly leathery. Bake in the oven for 15–20 minutes, or until the macaroons have formed a crisp shell and base.

7 Slide the baking parchment onto a cool surface, to encourage the bases of the macaroons to release from the paper. Leave to cool completely before peeling carefully from the paper. They will keep for a few days, stored in an airtight container.

8 To serve, sandwich the macaroons together in pairs with either a chocolate ganache, buttercream or jam.

Colour and flavour variations

❈ **Lemon** Use yellow food colouring. Sandwich the macaroons together with lemon curd.

❈ **Raspberry** Use red food colouring. Sandwich the macaroons together with raspberry ganache: mix 100g melted white chocolate with 50g warmed raspberry purée and cool for at least an hour before using. Alternatively, use 30g warmed raspberry purée and a few drops of raspberry essence.

❈ **Chocolate** Use brown food colouring. Sandwich the macaroons together with chocolate ganache (see page 153).

❈ **Coffee** Use brown food colouring. Sandwich the macaroons together with coffee butter icing (see page 152).

❈ **Vanilla** Omit the food colouring. Sandwich the macaroons together with vanilla butter icing (see page 152).

❈ **Pistachio nut** Use green food colouring. Sandwich the macaroons together with white chocolate and pistachio ganache: warm 50ml double cream with 1 tbsp pistachio paste, add to 100g melted white chocolate, stirring well, then leave to cool for at least an hour before using.

PINE NUT SABLÉS

MAKES about 30

85g pine nuts, plus extra to
finish (optional)
85g unsalted butter, softened
30g caster sugar, plus a little
extra to sprinkle

30g icing sugar
125g plain flour
½ tsp baking powder
Pinch of salt

These delicate, buttery biscuits have a lovely fine, sandy texture. Enjoy them with tea or coffee, or as an accompaniment to creamy desserts.

1 Heat the oven to 170°C/gas mark 3. Line a baking sheet ith baking parchment.

2 Spread the pine nuts out on a separate baking sheet and toast in the oven for 8–10 minutes, or until the nuts are lightly browned. Check after 5 minutes, as they can burn very easily. Remove from the oven and transfer to a plate to cool.

3 Reserve a few nuts for decorating the sablés and finely chop the remainder. Set aside.

4 Using a wooden spoon, cream the butter in a bowl until smooth. Add the caster and icing sugars and beat until pale and fluffy.

5 Sift the flour, baking powder and salt together twice to make sure they are really well combined. Add to the butter mixture, together with the chopped pine nuts, and mix thoroughly to form a soft dough.

6 Roll teaspoonfuls of the mixture into balls and place on the prepared baking sheet. Press them lightly with the palm of your hand to form rounds about 1cm high.

7 Press a few whole pine nuts on top of each sablé and sprinkle lightly with caster sugar. Bake in the middle of the oven for 20–30 minutes until pale golden. Remove from the oven and transfer to a wire rack to cool.

COCONUT TUILES

MAKES 20–25

35g butter, softened
85g caster sugar

1 egg, at room temperature
85g desiccated coconut

. . . .

To shape these delicate biscuits, you'll need a stencil. We simply use the lid of an empty plastic ice-cream container, with a round cut out, as the plastic is just the right thickness for the raw tuile mixture. This recipe produces flat biscuits, but you can shape the more traditional curved tuiles if you prefer (see note). The uncooked mixture can be stored in the fridge for up to a week and used as required.

1 Heat the oven to 170°C/gas mark 3 and line 2 baking sheets with non-stick baking parchment.

2 Using a hand-held electric whisk or a wooden spoon, cream the butter and sugar together in a medium bowl until just combined. Take care not to over-beat the mixture, or too much air will be incorporated.

3 Break the egg into a small bowl and beat lightly with a fork until broken up. Gradually add the egg to the creamed butter and sugar, in a few additions, beating well after each addition. Add the coconut and stir well to combine.

4 Using a 7cm diameter stencil (or a size of your choice) cut out from a plastic ice-cream container type lid, spread a thin and even layer of the mixture onto the lined baking sheets using a palette knife. Repeat this until the baking sheet is full, ensuring there is a little space in between each to allow for spreading. Bake in the oven until lightly golden and just set.

5 Carefully remove the tuiles from the parchment, using a palette knife, and place on a wire rack to cool. Store in an airtight container for up to 3 days.

. . . .

To shape traditional tuiles...

✷ You will need to bake the tuiles in small batches. While still warm and pliable from the oven, drape the discs over a rolling pin, to form into a slightly curved shape. Once the shape has set, remove them carefully to a wire rack to cool. If the tuiles cool too much before shaping, return them to the oven for a few minutes to soften and make pliable, but be aware that you cannot do this many times or they will eventually become very brittle and break very easily.

CHEWY DOUBLE CHOCOLATE COOKIES

MAKES 12 very large cookies	
100g milk chocolate	1 tbsp treacle
1 egg	250g plain flour
160g unsalted butter, softened	Pinch of salt
140g soft dark brown sugar	¼ tsp baking powder
100g granulated sugar	100g dark chocolate drops

The dough for these cookies can be made in advance and stored in the fridge for up to 3 days, so you could be barely 20 minutes away from freshly baked cookies at any time of the day or night!

1 Place 2 oven shelves in the top and bottom third of the oven, and line 2 baking sheets with baking parchment.

2 Chop the milk chocolate into about 1cm chunks and set aside. Break the egg into a small bowl and beat with a fork to loosen.

3 Put the butter in a large bowl and, using an electric whisk on a slow speed, cream for 30 seconds, or until smooth and well broken down. Add the sugars and treacle and continue to mix for a few minutes until the mixture becomes slightly paler and fluffy. Beat in the egg in 2 batches, until just combined.

4 Sift the flour, salt and baking powder together over the mixture and stir them in. Once combined, stir through the chopped chocolate and the chocolate drops, until all the ingredients are evenly incorporated.

5 Form the dough into 2 large sausages, 5cm in diameter, wrap each one in cling film and refrigerate for 20–30 minutes until firm enough to slice (or longer, if more convenient).

6 Heat the oven to 170°C/gas mark 3.

7 Cut one dough sausage into 6 even-sized discs. Lay 3 discs on each baking sheet, leaving at least 6cm space in between them, as they will spread (these are very large cookies).

8 Place the baking sheets on the pre-arranged shelves in the oven and bake for 10–14 minutes. Halfway through the cooking time, swap the baking sheets over, turning them 180° as you do so, to ensure even cooking. The cookies are cooked when they are lightly golden and just starting to set in shape, with no obvious raw dough remaining. They will still appear soft, but will firm up on cooling; it is important not to over-bake them, or they will lose their chewiness.

9 Remove from the oven and leave the cookies to cool for 2 minutes before transferring them to a wire rack to cool completely. Repeat the baking process with the second batch.

PEANUT BUTTER COOKIES

MAKES 12 very large cookies

70g unsalted peanuts
2 eggs, at room temperature
225g unsalted butter,
   softened
170g granulated sugar
170g soft dark brown sugar

1 tsp treacle
225g crunchy peanut butter
2 drops of vanilla extract
90g plain flour
1 tsp salt
2 tsp baking powder

These are chewy, indulgent and delicious – everything you could ask for in a cookie!

1 Heat the oven to 170°C/gas mark 3 and place 2 oven shelves in the top and bottom third of the oven. Line 2 baking sheets with baking parchment.

2 Put the peanuts into a roasting tin and toast in the oven for 10 minutes until very lightly coloured. Remove from the oven, tip onto a plate and set aside to cool, before roughly chopping.

3 Break the eggs into a small bowl and beat using a fork to break them up.

4 Using an electric whisk on a slow speed, cream the butter in a large bowl for 30 seconds, or until smooth and well broken down. Add the sugars and treacle and continue to mix for a few minutes until the mixture becomes slightly paler and fluffy.

5 Beat in the egg in several additions, beating after each addition until just combined. Add the peanut butter and vanilla and beat in as briefly as possible, until just combined. Sift the flour, salt and baking powder over the creamed mixture and stir them in.

6 Form the dough into 2 large sausages, 5cm in diameter, wrap each one in cling film and refrigerate for 30–60 minutes until firm enough to slice.

7 Cut one dough sausage into 6 even-sized slices. Arrange 3 slices on each baking sheet, ensuring that they are at least 6cm apart as they will spread (these are very large cookies), and press down to lightly flatten. Sprinkle with a few of the toasted peanuts, place the baking sheets on the pre-arranged shelves in the oven and bake for 10–15 minutes. Halfway through the cooking time, swap the baking sheets over, turning them 180° as you do so to ensure even cooking.

8 The cookies are done when they are lightly golden and just starting to set in shape with no obvious raw dough remaining; they will still appear soft, but will firm up upon cooling. Do not over-bake them, or they will lose their chewiness.

9 Remove from the oven and leave the cookies to cool for 2 minutes, before transferring them to a wire rack to cool completely. Repeat the baking process with the second batch.

SEVILLE ORANGE AND CHOCOLATE CHUNK COOKIES

MAKES 16	
250g good quality dark chocolate, about 70% cocoa solids	1 tbsp good quality cocoa powder
3 tbsp coarse-cut Seville orange marmalade	120g unsalted butter, softened
180g self-raising flour, plus extra to dust	60g soft light brown sugar
	1 large orange

Vary the flavour and texture of these cookies by using different types of marmalade, or by adding a tablespoon or two of chopped, toasted nuts, such as pecans or hazelnuts.

1 Line 2 baking trays with baking parchment.

2 Chop half the chocolate into small pieces, and the remaining half roughly. Set aside separately. Roughly chop the marmalade, or snip the shreds into smaller pieces with kitchen scissors and set aside in a bowl until needed.

3 Sift the flour and cocoa powder together into a bowl.

4 Cream the butter and sugar together in a medium bowl, using a wooden spoon, until pale and fluffy. Do not over-beat the mixture or you will incorporate too much air, which will make the dough very soft and likely to spread during baking.

5 Put the finely chopped chocolate in a small heatproof bowl set over a saucepan of just-boiled water, ensuring the bowl is not touching the water. Give the chocolate an occasional stir, to encourage it to melt. Finely grate the orange zest.

6 Stir the melted chocolate into the creamed butter mixture. Add the marmalade, roughly chopped chocolate, orange zest and flour and cocoa mixture to the bowl, and stir everything together until well combined. The dough should be quite firm.

7 Divide the dough into 16 equal portions and, with lightly floured hands, shape each piece into a ball. Arrange them on the baking sheets, leaving a space between each to allow for spreading, and press into flattish rounds, using your fingertips. Chill in the fridge for 15 minutes. Heat the oven to 180°C/gas mark 4.

8 Bake the cookies in the middle of the oven for 10–15 minutes, or until dry to the touch. Remove from the oven and leave to cool on the baking sheets for 5 minutes, then transfer to a wire rack to cool completely.

TAMARIND COOKIES

MAKES about 20	
1½ tbsp tamarind pulp	1 egg
2 tbsp boiling water	160g plain flour
1 lime	¼ tsp baking powder
125g butter, softened	Large pinch of ground star
150g soft light brown sugar	anise, to taste

This is a lovely way to enjoy the fruity sourness of tamarind. Leave out the star anise if you are not keen on an aniseed flavour. You could also make tiny tamarind biscuits to eat as petits fours after a fresh Asian-inspired meal.

1 Heat the oven to 180°C/gas mark 4. Line 2 baking sheets with baking parchment.

2 Chop the tamarind pulp, put into a bowl, pour the boiling water over and leave to soak for about 20 minutes, then press through a sieve, discarding the residue left in the sieve. Finely grate the lime zest.

3 Using an electric whisk, cream the butter and sugar together in a large bowl until light and fluffy. Break the egg into a small bowl and beat using a fork to loosen. Gradually beat the egg into the butter and sugar using the electric whisk, beating well between additions.

4 Sift the flour, baking powder and star anise over the creamed mixture, then fold in the strained tamarind pulp and lime zest until well combined.

5 Place half tablespoonfuls of the mixture on the prepared baking sheets, spacing them 4cm apart as they will spread.

6 Bake in the middle of the oven for 12–15 minutes, or until the cookies are browning round the edges, but still chewy and soft in the middle.

7 Remove from the oven and leave to cool on the sheets for 1–2 minutes before transferring to a wire rack to cool.

OATMEAL AND RAISIN COOKIES

MAKES about 20

100g raisins
120g butter
75g caster sugar
75g soft light brown sugar

1 large egg
1 tsp vanilla extract
100g self-raising flour
250g rolled oats

This chewy cookie recipe is very quick and simple to prepare, so make a batch for unexpected guests or as a 'pick me up' on a chilly weekend afternoon.

1 Heat the oven to 180°C/gas mark 4. Line 2 large baking sheets with baking parchment.

2 Put the raisins in a small bowl, pour on about 50ml boiling water and set aside to plump up while you make the dough.

3 Beat the butter and sugars together, using an electric whisk, until pale and fluffy. Beat the egg in another bowl with a fork and stir in the vanilla extract. Gradually whisk the egg into the butter mixture.

4 Sift in the flour and stir in well, using a spatula. Add the oats, with a drop of water if the mixture is too stiff to stir easily. Drain the raisins and stir them in too, discarding the liquid.

5 Drop tablespoonfuls of the mixture onto the prepared baking sheets, spacing them at least 4cm apart as the mixture will spread. Pat them down so they are slightly flattened.

6 Bake in the middle of the oven for 15–20 minutes, or until browning round the edges but still soft and chewy in the middle. Halfway through the cooking time, swap the top and bottom trays around in the oven, and at the same time turn the trays round so the back of the tray comes to the front, to ensure even cooking.

7 Remove from the oven and leave the cookies to set for 1–2 minutes before carefully transferring them to a wire rack to cool. They will keep for a few days in an airtight container.

CHOCOLATE AND PISTACHIO BISCOTTI

MAKES about 25

Oil, to grease
40g shelled, unsalted
   pistachios
40g good quality dark
   chocolate, minimum 60%
   cocoa solids
2 large eggs, plus 1 extra
   white

225g plain flour
Pinch of salt
½ tsp baking powder
70g granulated sugar
20g ground almonds

· ·

These biscuits are very dry and crisp – designed to be dipped into after-dinner liqueurs such as Amaretto or sweet Italian wines. Chopped dried fruit can be used in place of the chocolate, and chopped dried apricots in particular look great with the green of the pistachio.

1 Heat the oven to 190°C/gas mark 5. Lightly oil a large baking sheet.

2 Spread the pistachios out on the baking sheet and toast in the oven for about 8 minutes until just starting to colour. Tip onto a plate and leave to cool completely. Chop the chocolate into small pieces.

3 Beat the whole eggs in a small bowl with a fork, to break them up well.

4 Sift the flour, salt and baking powder into a large bowl. Stir in the sugar, chocolate, cooled pistachios and ground almonds and mix well.

5 Make a well in the centre of the dry ingredients, add the beaten eggs and gradually incorporate them into the dry ingredients, using a wooden spoon, to create a firm dough.

6 Divide the dough into 2 equal pieces and roll each piece into a long sausage shape, about 2cm in diameter and 20cm long. Place the rolls on the baking sheet at least 5cm apart.

7 Lightly whisk the remaining egg white and brush over the tops of the rolls. Bake in the middle of the oven for 20 minutes, then remove from the oven and reduce the oven temperature to 80°C/gas mark ¼.

8 Cut the rolls on a 45° angle into 1cm slices and spread out over the baking sheet (you may need a second sheet). Bake in the oven for 30 minutes to dry out, then turn the biscotti over and bake for a further 1 hour until completely dried out.

9 Remove from the oven and transfer to a wire rack to cool completely. Store in airtight jars.

VANILLA
BUTTER ICING

MAKES enough to ice a 20cm cake

125g butter, softened
200g icing sugar

A few drops of vanilla extract

This effortless soft butter icing is suitable for filling and topping all kinds of cakes.

1 Put the butter into a medium bowl and, using a hand-held electric whisk, cream until light and fluffy.

2 Sift in the icing sugar and add the vanilla extract. Whisk again for 5–7 minutes, or until the icing is light and fluffy.

Variations

✳ **Coffee butter icing** Replace the vanilla extract with 3 tsp finely ground strong espresso coffee (powder fine).

✳ **Chocolate butter icing** Mix 2 tbsp sifted cocoa powder with just enough boiling water to make a paste and allow to cool. Mix with the butter before adding the icing sugar and vanilla.

BUTTERCREAM

MAKES enough to fill and top a 22cm two-layered sponge

3 egg whites
175g icing sugar
120g unsalted butter,
   at room temperature

120g salted butter,
   at room temperature

This light, soft buttercream combines a meringue with a mix of unsalted and salted butters.

1 Put the egg whites and icing sugar in a large heatproof bowl and set over a saucepan of just simmered water (off the heat), making sure the base of the bowl is not touching the water.

2 Whisk until the meringue is thick and holding its shape, using a hand-held electric whisk. Remove the bowl from the pan of water and continue to whisk until the bowl is a little cooler.

3 Using a wooden spoon or hand-held electric whisk, beat the butters in a separate bowl. Gradually add the meringue, beating well after each addition, starting with 1 tbsp, then increasing the amount as you add more until it is all incorporated.

Flavourings

✳ **Lemon, orange or lime** To the finished buttercream, add the finely grated zest and juice of 1 lemon or orange, or 2 limes, to taste (the juice must not be cold).

✳ **Coffee** Stir 3–4 tsp warm very strong coffee or espresso, to taste, into the finished buttercream. (Alternatively, 40–50ml Camp Coffee can be used.)

✳ **Chocolate** Melt 75–85g good quality dark chocolate and stir thoroughly into the finished buttercream, in a few additions.

CHOCOLATE GANACHE

MAKES enough to fill two 22cm cakes generously

350g good quality dark
chocolate, minimum
60% cocoa solids

250ml double cream

· ·

Chocolate ganache is most often used as a filling for cakes. The consistency of ganache depends on the proportion of double cream to chocolate.

1 Chop the chocolate into small pieces, ideally about 1cm in size, and put into a heatproof bowl.

2 Pour the cream into a small saucepan and bring to a simmer over a medium heat. Slowly pour the hot cream over the chocolate pieces and stir gently until the chocolate has melted and the mixture is well combined.

3 Leave to cool until it begins to thicken a little around the edges, then beat with a hand-held electric whisk on a slow speed for 1–2 minutes until thickened a little but still creamy. Do not aerate the mixture too much.

PRALINE

MAKES 300g

Oil, to grease
150g blanched almonds

150g caster sugar

· ·

Praline is very versatile and an important ingredient in many classic cakes. Use shards of praline to decorate puddings, or grind to a powder to decorate cakes or to stir into ice creams or cream puddings.

1 Very lightly oil a baking sheet.

2 Put the almonds and sugar in a heavy-based sauté or frying pan and set over a low heat. As the sugar begins to melt and brown, use a fork to very gently encourage the unmelted sugar to the sides of the pan to melt and caramelise.

3 When the almonds start to make a cracking sound and all the sugar is a rich golden colour, tip the mixture onto the oiled baking sheet and flatten using the fork. Set aside to cool completely and harden.

4 Once cooled and hardened, the praline can be broken into pieces or pounded with a pestle and mortar or in a food processor to a fine or coarse powder, according to how you intend to use it.

EQUIPMENT

It is worth investing in the correct sized tin when you make a cake for the first time, as it will make a difference to the final result. Before long you will have built up a collection of the most useful tin sizes.

Equipment

Trays and tins for baking do not need to be non-stick, but should be solid enough not to warp when they are heated.

Scales A set of good scales is imperative – electronic scales are more accurate when measuring smaller quantities

Chopping boards Use separate boards for raw and cooked foods

Bowls A selection of various sizes, glass or stainless steel

Measuring jug

Juicer

Cake tins 20cm, 22cm sandwich tins; 20cm, 22cm, 23cm and 24cm springform tins; 18cm, 23cm and 25cm deep round cake tins; 22–23cm square tin; 30 x 20cm, 42 x 30cm Swiss roll tins

Silicone moulds Such as Madeleine and barquette moulds

Moule a manqué Tin with sloping sides

Baking sheets Some flat, some lipped

Shallow baking tins Selection of sizes

Roasting tins Selection of sizes

Wire cooling racks

Muffin tins

Mini-muffin tins

Loaf tin 450–500g, 900g–1kg

Flan ring 15cm (baseless)

Oven gloves

Utensils

Good kitchen tools make work in the kitchen easier and more efficient. The following are particularly useful:

Measuring spoons

Wooden spoons

Rolling pin

Kitchen scissors (a sturdy pair)

Swivel vegetable peeler

Apple corer

Pastry cutters

Palette knife

Spatula (heat resistant)

Fine grater

Zester

Pans

Saucepans At least 3 in a range of sizes from 18–28cm

Frying pans At least 2 in different sizes, from 16–28cm

Knives

Large cook's knife Important for fine slicing, fine chopping and many other food preparation tasks

Paring knife For controlled cutting of small ingredients

Pastry knife A long serrated knife is used for cutting cakes (also pastries and breads) without crumbling or tearing

Small serrated knife This is very useful for preparing fruit

Small electrical equipment

Electric mixer A free-standing mixer is perfect for mixing creamed cakes or whisking meringues

Hand-held electric whisk Creams together butter and sugar very swiftly. Also good for making meringues

Blender, hand-held stick blender, food processor Useful for purées and fruit coulis

Paper/lining products

Greaseproof paper

Baking parchment/silicone paper

Aluminium foil

Cling film

Non-stick baking mats (re-usable)

GLOSSARY

BALL STAGE, SOFT-/HARD Stages of sugar syrup boiling. To test, a little of the boiled sugar syrup is dropped into cold water. At 115°C it will form a soft ball; at 120°C it will form a hard ball.

BEURRE NOISETTE Butter cooked until it turns nut brown in colour, which happens when the milk solids caramelise.

BLOOM White sugar or fat deposits on the surface of chocolate, often because it has been kept in an environment that is too moist or too warm; the chocolate is still usable.

BOIL To cook food submerged in liquid heated so that the bubbles are constant and vigorous.

BROWN To bake (or roast or fry) to achieve colour and flavour as the natural sugars caramelise, such as the surface of a cake.

CARAMEL Sugar turned to a deep terracotta brown by heating.

CARAMELISE See Brown (above).

CHILL To cool food down in the fridge or using an ice bath, ideally to 4°C.

CLARIFIED BUTTER Butter which has been heated and the milk solids removed. This gives it a clear appearance and allows it to be heated to a high temperature without burning, while retaining the flavour of butter.

COULIS A thin purée, usually of fruit with a little sugar syrup.

CREAM To beat together ingredients in order to incorporate air, typically butter and sugar for a cake mixture.

CURDLE A mixture curdles when an emulsion separates undesirably. A cake mixture will curdle if it has been creamed insufficiently to absorb the egg once it it added, for example.

DROPPING CONSISTENCY When a mixture, such as a Victoria sponge mixture, will drop reluctantly from a spoon if it is tapped on the side of the bowl or pan, neither pouring off nor continuing to stick to the spoon.

EMULSION A suspension of fat and other liquid, such as a creamed cake mixture where the liquid from the beaten egg is suspended in the creamed butter and sugar mixture, for example.

FOLD To combine two or more mixtures using a large metal spoon or spatula and a lifting and turning motion to avoid destroying the air bubbles. Usually one of the mixtures is more airy and delicate than the other.

GLAZE To lend a glossy finish to a cake after baking, such as an apricot glaze brushed over a warm tea loaf on removing from the oven.

INFUSE To immerse aromatic ingredients such as herbs or spices in a hot liquid to flavour it.

LIGHTEN To incorporate air into a dish, by carefully folding in egg whites or lightly whipped cream for example.

LOOSEN When combining whisked egg whites into a heavier mixture, to first stir in a spoonful of the whisked whites to lighten the mixture before folding in the remainder.

NEEDLESHREDS Finely and evenly cut shreds of citrus zest, typically used as a garnish.

PASS To push a purée or soft ingredients through a sieve to achieve a fine texture.

PINCH An approximate quantity that can be pinched between the thumb and forefinger, less than 1/8 tsp.

PITH The soft white layer directly beneath the coloured zest of citrus fruit. It is invariably bitter in flavour and avoided when zesting the fruit.

POACH To completely submerge food in liquid that is hot yet barely trembling (certainly not bubbling), either on the hob or in the oven. Ideal for cooking delicate food.

PURÉE Usually vegetables or fruit, blended and/ or sieved until smooth. Purées can also be made from meat and fish.

REDUCE To rapidly boil a liquid in order to concentrate the flavour by evaporating some of the liquid.

RELAX OR REST To set a mixture aside in a cool place to facilitate a process. In the case of a batter, this allows the starch cells to swell, which results in a lighter cooked result.

RIBBON STAGE When a whisked egg or mousse mixture is thick enough to leave a line or ribbon over the surface when the whisk is lifted and some of the mixture falls from it is described as the ribbon stage or 'to the ribbon'.

ROAST To cook uncovered, without added liquid, in the oven.

RUB IN To rub small pieces of butter into flour with the fingertips until the mixture resembles breadcrumbs.

SCALD To heat a liquid (milk, usually) until on the verge of boiling. At scalding point, steam is escaping and bubbles are starting to form around the edge of the pan.

SETTING POINT The stage at which a mixture containing gelatine starts to set. Also the point where the pectin gels in jams and jellies, which should then be removed from the heat.

SIMMER To cook food submerged in liquid, heated to a level that ensures small bubbles constantly appear around the edge of the pan.

SLAKE To mix a thickening ingredient such as cornflour with a little cold water and then whisk the mixture into the sauce to thicken it. Unstable ingredients such as yoghurt should also be slaked into a mixture using a little of the sauce, to prevent curdling.

SPONGE Soaking powdered gelatine in a little water until it forms a translucent spongy gel before melting.

STEAM To cook food in hot vapour, usually from boiling water. This is a gentle method of cooking food, which sits in a perforated container or permeable bamboo steamer and cooks in the steam that surrounds it. Alternatively, in indirect steaming, the food is protected from the steam itself but cooks in the heat created by it; a steamed sponge enclosed in a covered pudding basin is an example.

SYRUPY The consistency of a sauce reduced down until it just coats the back of a spoon. Similar to warm syrup or honey.

THREAD STAGE An early stage of sugar syrup boiling. To test, a little of the boiled sugar syrup is dropped into cold water, then removed and pulled between the finger and thumb. At 110°C it will form a fine thread as it is pulled.

WELL A hollow in a mound of flour in a bowl or on the work surface, created to contain the liquid ingredients before they are incorporated. Used in batter making.

ZEST The coloured outer skin of citrus fruit used for flavouring, which must be carefully removed from the bitter white pith before it is added. 'To zest' describes the action of finely paring the zest.

INDEX

··

ACKNOWLEDGEMENTS

The recipes in this book have been compiled, adapted and edited by Jenny Stringer, Claire Macdonald and Camilla Schneideman, but the authors are a large collection of Leiths staff and visiting teachers, past and present. Thank you to everyone who wrote recipes for this book, notably: Mel Barnett, Fiona Burrell, Max Clark, Julie Gallagher, Sarah Hall, Caroline Jones, Claire Macdonald, Heli Miles, Shenley Moore, Sue Nixon, Mel Ryder, Camilla Schneideman, Valeria Sisti, Belinda Spinney, Jenny Stringer and Ron Sweetser.

But with the sheer number of talented cooks around us at the school, we must say a big thank you to everyone who has helped develop ideas for this book, tested the recipes (particularly Sarah Hall who undertook an intensive testing programme!) and given valuable feedback during the tasting sessions. Special thanks must go to Helene Robinson-Moltke, Ansobe Smal and Belinda Spinney who were at the photo shoots.

Thank you to the team at Quadrille. We have been extremely lucky to continue our relationship with our editor Janet Illsley. Janet's patience with the authors is legendary – deadlines with this number of people involved required military organisation and, as ever, we are incredibly grateful for her wisdom. Thank you too Sally Somers for editing the copy.

Thank you to the team that worked together on the design and photography for this book: Peter Cassidy for his brilliant photography, Gabriella Le Grazie for her art direction, and Emily Kydd and Emily Quah (both Leiths graduates) for the food styling. We are thrilled with the new style Katherine Keeble has created for this series of books, so thank you all.

CREATIVE DIRECTOR Helen Lewis
PROJECT EDITOR Janet Illsley
DESIGN Katherine Keeble
ART DIRECTION Gabriella Le Grazie
PHOTOGRAPHER Peter Cassidy
FOOD STYLISTS Emily Kydd and Emily Quah
LEITHS CONSULTANT Helene Robinson-Moltke, Ansobe Smal and Belinda Spinney
COPY EDITOR Sally Somers
PROPS STYLISTS Iris Bromet and Cynthia Inions
PRODUCTION Vincent Smith and Tom Moore

First published in 2015 by
Quadrille Publishing Limited
www.quadrille.co.uk

Text © 2015 Leiths School of Food and Wine
Photography © 2015 Peter Cassidy
Design and layout © 2015 Quadrille Publishing Limited

The rights of the author have been asserted.

Cataloguing in Publication Data: a catalogue record for this book is available from the British Library.

ISBN 978 184949 5493

Printed in China